THE CIVIL
in the Trent Valley

Andrew Polkey

© 1992

ISBN 0 946404 92 5

Printed and Published by
J. H. Hall & Sons Limited, Siddals Road, Derby
Printers and Stationers since 1831
Telephone: Derby (0332) 45218
Facsimile: (0332) 296146

 THE DERBYSHIRE HERITAGE SERIES

. . . . an unthinkable war between families, between communities and localities; this being the story of warfare in one small region of the kingdom . . . .

INTRODUCTION

Sir John Gell (1593-1671) from an original engraving held in Derby Local Studies Library

It is impossible to reconstruct anything of the events of the Civil War in Derbyshire without at once coming into immediate contact with the remarkable personality of Sir John Gell (1593-1671) of Hopton Hall near Wirksworth. Were it not for his decisive military intervention in October 1642 — when he established a Parliamentary garrison at Derby — then Derbyshire (and possibly Nottinghamshire too) would readily have fallen to the King. It was Gell alone who, in a predominantly Royalist county, first openly rallied to the cause of Parliament and raised a regiment of foot and then in 1643 a regiment of horse, to harry and disperse his more leaden-footed Royalist rivals. It was his character alone — ruthless, authoritarian and vindictive — which ensured that whilst the fortunes of war swirled and eddied across the region of the North Midlands, Derby remained a Parliamentarian island, a springboard from which, after the great Royalist defeat at Marston Moor, he was able to launch Parliamentarian counter-offensives against the local Royalist garrisons which were dotted throughout the Peak District and along the Trent valley.

As one local historian has written:

'Gell's career in itself would fill a book; indeed, a full-length biography is probably overdue . . . his activities bulk so large in the county's affairs that the events of 1642-1646 were effectively controlled and directed by him. Of necessity, therefore, the history of that period largely parallels Gell's own. After 1646 his involvement ceases, but no other single figure appears thereafter to dominate the county scene. Gell stands head and shoulders above the rest as the dynamo of Parliamentary activity, and his departure leaves one with a sense almost of anti-climax, so vigorous and pervasive is his presence.' *(Brian Stone).*

With an income of at least £3,000 a year, based largely on land and lucrative lead-mining interests in the Wirksworth area, by 1642 he was one of the wealthiest gentlemen of the county. He served as a Captain of Foot in the Derbyshire trained bands, was a Presbyterian in religion (but certainly no Puritan) and by the 1630s was identified with the growing opposition to Charles's religious and fiscal policies. He contracted marriage settlements for his children with a number of future anti-Royalist families and around 1635/6 was prudent enough to settle his estates on his son John, reserving for himself a small annuity for life. He would certainly not have done so without premeditated cause and as a possible precaution against the future. He was no friend to the King.

It was perhaps for this very reason that he was deliberately selected by the government to serve as the first sheriff in 1635 to collect the notorious Ship Money tax in Derbyshire. It might have seemed that royal policy had succeeded in detaching him from the growing opposition, for he startled both sides by the unexpected and muscular efficiency which he brought to this controversial task. No objectors were safe and he alienated friend and foe alike by his rigorous exactions. He used his power to harass and oppress those against whom he had a grudge — in particular the Stanhope family — and certainly exceeded his authority by actually managing to collect an excess of the tax in the county. A flurry of petitions came down from Derbyshire to the Commissioners protesting against Gell's overbearing prosecution of his office. As a belated reward, in 1642, Charles created him a baronet, yet failed in the last resort to attract him to the ranks of the nascent Royalist party.

Gell's unexpected reversion to the cause of Parliament in October 1642 therefore remains a partial mystery. Perhaps he simply saw the shrievalty as a means of financial self-advancement and nothing more — hence the 'surplusage' which he confessed to having amassed when writing to the Commissioners — but Lucy Hutchinson, (no friend of Gell's), had a more cynical explanation:

'He had by many aggravating circumstances not only

4

concerning his prosecution of Sir John Stanhope, but others, so highly misdemeaned himself that he looked for punishment from the parliament. To prevent it he very early put himself into their service.'

A more comprehensible interpretation is advanced by Trevor Brighton, who suggests that Gell's pre-war associations — whatever he did as sheriff in 1635 — unmistakably rank him amongst the county's opposition party. More pertinently, to a man with Gell's known penchant for the pursuit of vendettas, he joined Parliament's service because the hated Stanhope family 'were Royalists to a man.' Gell's subsequent unsavoury treatment of the Stanhopes throughout the war certainly appears to justify this theory.

Whether for fear or favour, Gell's espousal of the Parliamentarian cause was a decisive event and had direct and long-term consequences for the way in which military events unfolded in the North Midlands. It is high time that the role Gell played and the contribution he made to Parliament's war effort, should reach a wider audience and receive some appreciation and detailed analysis by all who would describe themselves as students of the English Civil War.

PART I

THE FIRST MOVES

22 AUGUST 1642 — NOTTINGHAM

King Charles raised his standard and called all loyal citizens to join him in suppressing the rebellion instigated by factious elements within the Parliament. Support was slow in forthcoming so on 13th September the small army set out on a

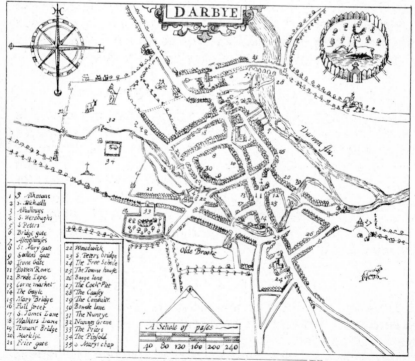

John Speed's map of Derby 1610 — courtesy of Derby Library

march to Shrewsbury to recruit. Two days later it reached Derby and Charles borrowed £300 from the bewildered corporation and departed, reinforced by only a handful of citizens. Sir John Gell had meanwhile thought it prudent to leave Derbyshire and on 27th at Worcester received a commission from the Earl of Essex, the commander of the main Parliamentarian field army, to raise a regiment of foot. Armed with this and determined to fill the void left by the King's march to Shrewsbury, Gell and his brother Thomas hastened to Hull where they had been promised a company of grey-coated London volunteers with which to form the nucleus of a Derby regiment.

Moving from Hull to Chesterfield by the 17th October, Gell managed to raise a further 200 men and then reached his home territory at Wirksworth in time to scatter a party of Royalist foragers under Sir Francis Whortley. News that the first great battle of the Civil War had been inconclusively fought on 23nd October at Edgehill between the King and Essex, indicated that the war would not be won by a sudden knock-out blow. Instead, local forces would have to seize towns and territory and squeeze out their opponents.

31 OCTOBER 1642 — DERBY

Gell therefore acted swiftly and descended on Derby. He entered the town unopposed and began to create a garrison. He recruited further local men to add to the core of Londoners and received a welcome supply of muskets sent up from London via the powerful Parliamentarian base at Hull. Sir George Gresley from Drakelow came over with a troop of horse and on 5th November Charles White from Nottingham- shire rode in with a party of dragoons to reinforce Gell's growing strength.

10 NOVEMBER 1642 — DALE

Whortley appeared at the village of Dale. Gell put his musketeers on horseback and sent them against Whortley, who promptly fled the county.

Gell meanwhile gave out commissions. His brother Thomas was made Lieutenant Colonel and one of Gell's tenants from

Wirksworth, a Dutchman named Molanus, was created Major. The Captains at this time were one Vermuyden — another Dutchman — John Mundy, and Thomas Sanders. Charles White was made Captain of Dragoons and George Gresley Captain of the Horse troop. Two more foot captains — Stafford and Mellor — were added later.

THE GELL COLOUR

The regiment was issued with colours, one per company, and remarkably, one of these survives today in the hands of Sir John's descendants and is one of only a handful of civil war flags still in existence. The colour is enclosed in glass for preservation and affixed to a wall above a stair well. Measurements are therefore approximate, being based on photographs taken by the author.

The flag is 6 foot high by 6 foot 6 inches wide. The main body of the cloth is made of 2 lengths of a Golden-yellow silk with a horizontal seam. The lower piece is 3 feet 6 inches high, the upper 2 feet 6 inches. On to this square has been sewn a canton, a cross of St. George in the top corner next to the pole. The canton is a two foot square piece of white silk with a cross made of two 7 inch wide strips, the vertical being sewn on first and overlaid by the horizontal band. The canton was completed prior to being attached to the main body of the flag. There is a separate canton on each side of the flag.

The sleeve could at most contain a 1.5 inch diameter pole. Two 15 inch gold cords which may not be original, are attached to the top of the sleeve and end in tassels.

The devices are dark blue, having been stencilled on.

There was another colour of this set in the late 19th century, as a watercolour shows, but its fate is unknown.

19 NOVEMBER 1642 — DERBY

Royalist agents acting for the Earl of Newcastle from Bolsover, secretly entered the town and tried to raise a riot. They were driven out by the townspeople and one was killed, evidence at this stage that the town of Derby was in Gell's grasp and strongly Parliamentarian in sympathy.

25 NOVEMBER 1642 COVENTRY

Gell records that on this date his regiment was 'compleate' but in all probability was something nearer 750 strong rather than the theoretical establishment of 1200.

He again mounted some 300 musketeers and sent them under Major Molanus with White's Dragoons as escort, to Coventry. Five days later they returned with 2 sakers and a supply of ammunition.

DECEMBER 1642 — BRETBY HOUSE

This was the seat of Philip Stanhope 1st Earl of Chesterfield and had been garrisoned for the King with 40 musketeers, 80 Horse and 7 drakes. Bretby was to be the first of many sieges in the County and doubtless this was the reason for the sakers being fetched from Coventry.

Molanus with 400 foot stormed the house after the sakers proved incapable of making a breach. Stanhope fled to Lichfield where he shut himself up in the Close and from which he was to be winkled out the following March. Meanwhile, Molanus possessed himself of the Earl's artillery whilst the soldiers plundered the house. Gell narrates how this came about in an uncharacteristic passage of exculpation contained in his 'A True Relation:'

'Wee, forsably entring the house, found his Countess, her gentlewoman and two or three servants therein, seized presently upon the arms, and found seven drakes, thirty steel pikes, twenty or thirty musquetts, five double barrells of powder and good store of match and bulletts. Major Molanus, Captayne White, Captayne Sanders and divers other officers entreated the Countess that shee would give every souldyer halfe a crowne, for to have her house saved from plundering, because it was a free boottey. Shee answered, it was too much, and that shee had not so much monyes; they asked her againe if shee would give amongst them forty marks: shee made the same answer, thet shee had not monyes. Then they offered to deposite the money for her, if shee would promise to repay them: she still refractoroly and willfully said that shee would not give them one penny; and then indeed the souldyers plundred the house. But the said officers saved her owne chamber, with all the goods therein.'

One must remember that this document was put together at the end of the war when Gell sought to recover his expenses laid out in the service of Parliament and to vindicate many of his more controversial actions. It is very much an example of special pleading and needs to be used with caution. Nevertheless, it is the chief source for a military account of Derbyshire in the Civil War and provides a narrative framework which can be corroborated by reference to less partizan sources.

'A True Account' also mentions the reprehensible sack of Bretby house and one may wonder why Gell took so many pains to excuse such a savage business so early on in the war. The fact is, Gell had a bitter feud with the Stanhopes which antedated the war. One can only conclude that his soldiers behaviour at Bretby was not accidental. In any event, this is how Gresley further explains the sacking:

' . . . we tooke the house and should have donne no more hurt, but only taken the armes and ammunition, if the Countess would have given the common souldiers £20 to drinke, which she refusing, part of the house was plundered, to which act the souldiers were more inclined, when they understoode that some of their fellowes taken prisoners at the first onsett had received hard usage, some of them having had the honour to be beaten by the Earle himself, whom his servants had first disarmed, and then held fast from styrring . . . '

NOTTINGHAM 1642

Shortly afterwards, Major Molanus and Captain White were sent to Nottingham with 300 foot to assist Colonel Pierrepont raise a regiment and garrison the Castle. They stayed there for some 9 or 10 days and helped to erect defences. White then left the Derby forces and his place as Captain of Dragoons was taken later by Daniel Watson, an incomer from Burton-on-Trent.

5 JANUARY 1643 — SWARKESTONE FIGHT

The Royalist commander, Henry Hastings, from his Castle at Ashby-de-la-Zouch in Leicestershire, provided a focus for those Derbyshire Royalists who had been outraged by Gell's seizure of the County town, by his treatment of Stanhope and by his generally rapacious behaviour. Whilst Gell's forces were employed at Nottingham, Hastings garrisoned the house of one of his Derbyshire officers — Sir John Harpur — at Swarkestone on the River Trent and also began to fortify the bridge itself. Gell was well aware that the River Trent provided

The Medieval causeway at Swarkestone Bridge and scene of the first significant encounter between Derbyshire's Royalists and Parliamentarians in January 1643.

a valuable line of defence between himself and the rising power of Hastings to the south. So fearing quite rightly that Hastings was preparing a springboard for the push against Derby, Gell summoned Molanus back from Nottingham and the whole regiment plus Gresley's Horse, threw itself against the Royalist barricades:

' . . . soe having two saccers along with him hee marched thither, stormed their workes, drove the enemy away, and dismantled the same, killed seven or eight of them and wounded many, and again but one man of his wounded, soe that the enemy never had a mind to fortifie the same againe.' (T.R.).

JANUARY 1643 — UTTOXETER

The Moorlanders of Staffordshire then approached Gell for assistance against Stafford and so Molanus and 200 foot were sent off to a rendezvous at Uttoxeter. However, the Moorlanders failed to turn up, so after 2 or 3 days, Molanus marched back to Derby. Gell's regiment was becoming a force to be reckoned with and this was but the start of an increasing number of requests for assistance from surrounding Parliamentarians. Although the Moorlanders proved to be an unreliable lot, officers and men from the Derby garrison were later sent to Leek to train and drill them.

17 JANUARY 1643 — ASHBY

The Roundhead commander in Leicester, Lord Grey and Sir William Brereton from Cheshire, combined with Gell for an attack on Hastings's base at Ashby. Their forces successfully stormed the town but the Royalists held out in the Castle. A siege was contemplated, but supposedly false intelligence that Prince Rupert had left Banbury with a relief force, caused the attackers to break off and retreat to Derby. Gell did not believe that the attempt to reduce Hastings should have been given up so lightly and remarked:

'Our regiment was appoynted to fall upon the towne, we beate the enemy out of the workes, tooke the towne and forced them to retyre into the mannor house and church; but presently after the Lord Grey, our commander in chiefe, had false intelligence of the comeing of Prince Rupert, which he too easily believed, and called us off, and so saved Hastings and the house, which otherwise had been yielded to us.' (T.A.).

In Derby, the Cheshire and Leicester forces remained a week much to Gell's chagrin, for 'they lost us and the towne £500.' This was money that Colonel Gell could ill afford to waste on such hungry and uncertain allies. But 'it was but a small loss in respect of what damage Hastings hath since done us; who hath ever been a thorn in our sydes.'

Having been baulked of his prey at Ashby, Gell sought to insulate himself from a resurgent Hastings by blocking off the only two other bridges over the Trent. Accordingly he sent forces to Nottingham where they 'sett out theyre workes, and stayed there untyll those workes were advanced,' and sent his largest company to guard the bridge at Burton-on-Trent. On the importuning of Fairfax, Essex ordered Gell to send some of his strength into Yorkshire; so from Swarkestone bridge, Captain Mundy's company was marched to Sheffield to assist in fortifying the Castle. Meanwhile Captain Stafford's company was at Whaleybridge, on the Cheshire border, guarding the north-west route into Derbyshire.

28 FEBRUARY 1643 — NEWARK

It was at this time that Essex ordered Gell to assist Major General Ballard in an attack on Newark. Molanus left his company at Burton, presumably under Captain Sanders, and with 500 foot from Derby, he joined Ballard's forces for the assault which took place on the 28th. This left only Captain Mellor's company and Gresley's troop of Horse to defend Derby.

The Derby foot were brigaded with the Notts foot on the south of the town under Colonel Hutchinson and acquitted themselves well, though the attack was beaten off by the garrison and gave rise to a welter of accusations and counter-accusations amongst the Parliamentarians. Molanus returned to Derby 'with the loss of some men and one drake.'

Gresley states clearly enough in his 'True Account' that the Derby gray-coats had beaten the Newarkers from their works and planted their colours there:

' . . . and when there was no other expectation but of takeing the towne, instead of being seconded we were called off, for some secret reason, which our commanders could never yet truly understand.'

2-5 MARCH 1643 — LICHFIELD

Upon the death of Lord Brooke, his Lieutenant Colonel, Sir Edward Peyto sent a Captain Fox to Derby to request that Sir John Gell take command of the forces besieging the Earl of Chesterfield in the Close. That he should have been asked to take up this command is a reflection both of his abilities and of the military reputation of the forces which he had raised at Derby, most of which were still serving at Newark when Fox arrived. Gell, of course, was more than happy to move against his old enemy, and hurried over to Lichfield leaving only Captain Mellor's Company to watch Derby in his absence.

Meanwhile, Peyto had collected wives, women and children belonging to the Royalist garrison in the Close and proceeded to drive them at the head of his troops as a human screen. The attack failed and Peyto himself was wounded. Though the Royalist broadsheets later blamed Gell for this decidedly unsporting behaviour, it would seem that he was still en route for the City at the time the attack was made.

Sir John had a more effective plan for breaking Stanhope's resistance, and sent for a mortar from Coventry. After a few bombs were lobbed into the Close, the Earl surrendered after a siege of only four days.

Sir William Brereton, who had arrived with Lord Brooke's forces, was clearly overshadowed at this stage in the war by the bellicose and victorious John Gell. All the more strange therefore to note that of this notable success, Gell himself has very little to say in either of the two accounts and simply states thet he 'gayned Litchfield cloase and sett all in good order.'

19 MARCH 1643 — HOPTON HEATH

Gell and Brereton agreed to make an attempt against Stafford and to that end arranged to unite their forces on

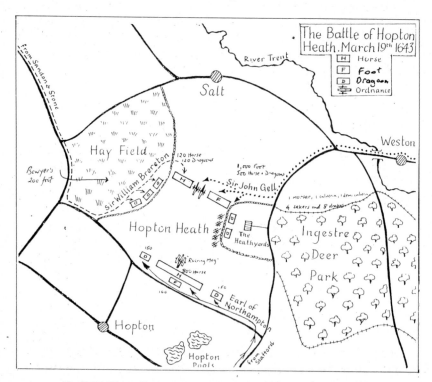

The Battle of Hopton Heath, map reproduced with acknowledgements to Trevor Brighton

Hopton Heath, a moorland ridge some 3 miles north-east of Stafford.

Gell had around 1,000 foot, which must have represented his entire command, together with a detachment from Brooke's regiment, plus some 500 or so Moorlanders who joined him on the march. He had besides a respectable train of 15 guns.

On the evening of the 17th an advance party of dragoons under Captain Watson entered the village of Great Haywood to prepare quarters for the rest of Gell's little army, which at that time was scattering into various villages to spend the night. However, the Royalists knew of Gell's movements and flushed Watson out with a sudden attack. Sir John then realised that the enemy were already in control of Stafford but he decided to wait nevertheless to keep his appointment with Brereton.

The resulting battle *(refer to map)* which took place on the 19th is well known and its outlines do not therefore need to be traced here. However, Gell's description of the fight, contained in the 'True Account' and the 'True Relation,' makes the following pertinent observations:

1. The enemy were far stronger then expected, 'above one thousand horse'. (TA) (1,200 in TR).

2. At the first charge of the Earl of Northampton's cavalry, 'all our horse fled, except about 240 of the Lord Brooke's reformader troupe, who behaved themselves all very gallantly.' (TA).

3. TR specifically comments on the Parliamentarian command structure, viz.
'Col. Gell commanded all the ffoot, and Sir William Brereton the horse.'

4. Upon the first Royalist charge, 'Sir William's horse presently ran away and left Sir John Gell alone with the ffoot.' (TR).

It need not be wondered at that the two Roundhead leaders failed hereafter to co-operate successfully again. From Sir John's point of view, the business at Ashby and then at

Lichfield had confirmed that Brereton could only play a subordinate role. And after the rout of Brereton's troops at Hopton Heath and their flight from the field, Gell was entitled to believe himself the better man of the two and thereafter made any kind of joint operation with Brereton a near impossibility. Brereton's greatness was yet to come, whereas, militarily speaking, Gell was enjoying perhaps his finest hour.

Graphically, Gresley describes the crisis of the battle:

(TA) 'Our Colonell quitt his horse, and went to the foote, being then in great feare and disorder, many of them readie to rune, and standing with theyre pykes advanced; the Colonell, with his owne hands, put down theyre pykes, encouraged both them and the musquetyers, who were all disorderly, crowded together; he speedely gott them into order and gave the enemie such a vollie of shott upon theyre chardge, that they first wheeled, and much discouraged by the death of the Earle of Northampton and Captaine Middleton, with dyvers others, gentlemen and officers, that all presently fledd . . '

Brereton's account of the battle gives the numbers of horse as 'not four hundred horse at the most, whereof I brought two troopes' plus five troops of dragoons 'whereof I brought three.' Furthermore, of the foot he states:

'I do not believe that all our foot there should present could make five hundred men.' Interestingly enough, he says nothing whatever of Gell's leadership or of his handling of the battle, other than to comment adversely on the way in which the forces were drawn up:

'It was a great disadvantage unto us, that both our horse and foote were unhappily disposed of and divided into small bodyes, at such time as the enemie charged us, which was the occasion that the greatest parte of our horse were discovered, and routed, and yet very few of them slaine.'

Instead, he attributes victory to the wisdom and goodness of Divine Providence and ignores Gell entirely, prefering to dwell on the performance of his dragoons . . . 'which did extraordinary good service. There were near one hundred of the dragoons slaine in the place where the dragoons skirmished; and I cannot discerne that we lost more than two or three. And yet they fought so long, and so fiercely, until all their powder and bullet was spent. Afterwards they joyned,

16

and fell to it pell mell, one upon another, with the stocks of their musketts.'

The Royalist losses are well known and included their commander, the Earl of Northampton, whose body was recovered from the field by Gell, but one cannot believe him when he says (TR) 'of our side, three carters and two souldyers were slayne.'

The worst loss of the day from Sir John's point of view, was the capture of his drakes, which had been overridden by the Royalist horse. This alone explains a macabre sequel to the battle, for when retreating via Uttoxeter to Derby over the following three days, he was approached by a trumpeter from the Earl's son requesting the return of his father's body for burial. Gell's response was to use the Earl's body as a bargaining counter with which to demand in exchange the return of his lost artillery. He also demanded the repayment of money paid to a surgeon for embalming the body! This unscrupulous episode reads like the account of a fictitious and 'Bloody Rebel' culled from a Royalist propaganda sheet, but is baldly and shamelessly set down by Sir John himself in his True Relation:

'There came a trumpetter to him from my younge Lord of Northampton for his father's dead body, whereupon hee answered, if hee would send him the drakes which they had gotten from their dragoons and pay the chirurgeons for embalming it, hee should have it: but hee returned him an answer, that hee would doe neither th' one nor th' other, and soe Colonell Gell caused him to be carried in his company to Derby, and buried him in the Earle of Devonshire's sepulcher in All Hallowes church.'

Such was the outrage occasioned by this dishonourable act, that when a week later, the King issued a general pardon to Staffordshire and Derbyshire, the names of Brereton and Gell were specifically excepted. The former of course, knew nothing of this and had disappeared back into Cheshire as darkness first fell over the carnage at Hopton Heath.

PART II

THE FIGHT FOR SURVIVAL

APRIL 1643 — SUTTON SCARSDALE

On 8th April, the very day when prince Rupert began his bombardment of the Roundhead garrison left at Lichfield, Gell learned that Francis Leake, Lord Deincourt, had fortified his house at Sutton Scarsdale and was sending assistance to the Earle of Newcastle's garrison at Bolsover. He despatched his brother, Lieutenant Colonel Thomas Gell, Major Molanus and Captain Sanders with 500 men and 3 guns to take the house. After a brief skirmish in which 2 or 3 men were killed, Deincourt surrendered and agreed to come to Derby within the week to compound and submit to Parliament. However, as soon as Gell's troops had destroyed the defences and marched away, Deincourt promptly fled to Newark where he remained till 1646. Gell was furious that Deincourt had so dishonourably broken his parole, calling him a 'lump of flesche' . . (that) . . 'will bee nether for service of Kinge nor Parliament.' But his real anger was caused by Deincourt reneging on his oath to pay Gell the sum of £4,000 to save his estate.

APRIL 1643 — BURTON ON TRENT

Until Rupert left Lichfield on 22nd April, Gell was busy trying to organise a relief expedition but his neighbours failed to co-operate. Outlying garrisons were called in as Derby prepared to receive the same treatment meted out to Colonel Russel when the Close was stormed on 20th. However, after the surrender, Rupert was called away to Oxford by the King and Gell was able to retaliate. He met with Lord Grey on

Egginton Heath mid-way between Derby and Burton-on-Trent and advanced against the latter to mop up the garrison left there after Rupert's departure. Its long Medieval bridge was strategically important, being 'the only passage over the Trent and Dove into the North' and Gell decided that the river line had to be held strongly against the resurgent Royalists and Colonel Bagot's new regiment based at Lichfield. Accordingly, he left Burton in the care of one of his biggest foot companies (200 men) under Captain Sanders, together with a gun and 60 dragoons.

MAY 1643 — DERBYSHIRE

The threat from Rupert at Lichfield was promptly replaced by the greater threat posed by the Earl of Newcastle's army in Yorkshire. As Gell puts it, 'Whilst these things were in actinge, the Earl of Newcastle grewe powerfull in the North.' At this time, Gell's brother Thomas was at Chesterfield with 2 foot companies and 2 small pieces of ordinance. In the confused situation that followed the taking of Rotherham, Thomas Gell fell back to Derby, pursued by the all-conquering Royalists. The area of territory held by Gell now shrank away to Derby itself:

'Newcastle's army was now victorious, he came on into our country, miserably plunders, and takes all before hym, leavies greate summies of money, and raiseth more men by the commission of array; we were again threatened, and expected daylie to be besieged, and, to speak ingenuously, we were never more in danger than at that instant.' (TA).

It was at this critical moment that the only remaining garrison, that of Captain Sanders at Burton, chose to defect. The details of what actually transpired are hard to determine, particularly as by this time Gell and Sanders cordially detested one another, but it appears that Sanders was persuaded by a Lancashire man, one Colonel Haughton, to join his regiment and become its Lieutenent Colonel, together with his entire command. Gell infers cowardice and self-interest as the motive, but the later career of Sanders argues strongly against such an over-simplistic interpretation. One may postulate perhaps, that after some 6 months service, the soldiers preferred their Captain to their Colonel and were heartily sick of the latter's vindictive and violent personality, of which more will be said at a later date.

In the event, Gell was saved; 'It pleased God to preserve us, and the Northern Popish army, in the height of theire pryde, were suddenly called back . . ' Fairfax stormed Wakefield on 21st May and Newcastle retreated in order to deal with him. Derbyshire would have to wait.

But Sir John had not been idle. Since the beginning of May he had been commanded by Lord Grey to attend a muster in the vale of Belvoir, where he was joined by the Leicestershire and Nottinghamshire forces, Colonel Cromwell and the young Hotham. Here they remained for some 7 weeks, awaiting the outcome of the struggle in the North. However, the sudden appearance of Queen Henrietta's army put them all to flight, although Gell argues valiantly that with 6,000 horse, he would have risked a battle. It was not to be and the Roundhead army broke up, Gell's horse making off to Leicester.

7 JULY 1643 — BURTON ON TRENT

The Queen's army moved from Newark to Ashby and then turned against Burton-on-Trent. Gell (TR) writes that he summoned the Staffs. and Notts. forces to meet him on Egginton Heath once more, 'and soe to Burton, to assist them till the Queene were past, but noebody would come, soe that within three days after she marched towards Burton, tooke the towne by storme, killed many of them, tooke the Colonel, (Haughton) Lieutenant Colonel (Sanders) and most of the officers prisoners, and soe most miserably plundered and destroyed the towne.'

Gresley relates (TA) that Sanders was exchanged in return for his promise 'to serve faithfully hereafter in this countrie' and that he should be promoted Major of the new regiment of horse that Essex had commissioned Gell to raise and to command as its Colonel.

From the moment the Queen's army left Newark on 3rd

July, Gell prepared for an expected attack on Derby. His troops were all called back from Nottingham and Leicester and Parliament sent some much needed supplies escorted into Derby by Captain Swetnam's troop of horse. The weaponry included 20 barrels of powder, 300 muskets, 60 carbines and 60 cases of pistols; so for the first time, Gell's regiment was fully armed. The defenders were not put to the test however, for the Queen passed on to Walsall where on July 8th she wrote to the King — 'If it had not been for your express command not to delay we should have been at Derby and certainly taken that town as well.'

8 JULY 1643 — WOOTTON LODGE

With Henrietta Maria's army out of the way, Gell's regiment emerged from Derby and launched into Staffordshire, to attack the fortified house of Sir Richard Fleetwood at Wootton Lodge, near Ellastone, six miles west of Ashbourne. Fleetwood had been imitating Henry Hastings at Ashby by robbing carriers travelling between Manchester and London. His garrison Gresley describes as — 'manned with such a company of obstinate papists, and resolute theeves, as the like were hardly to be found in the whole kingdome . . . ' (TA).

Swetnam's horse, Captain Mellor and Lieutenant Colonel Thomas Gell with 400 foot took the house after one day's fighting and brought Fleetwood and his 70-80 men, roped together, to Derby.

20 JULY 1643 — TUTBURY

It was now the turn of Hastings's garrison at Tutbury and Gell descended on the place with 'all his fforces, horses, and ffoot and artillery' . . in order to re-capture the Parliamentarians imprisoned there after surrender at Burton. He was accompanied by Sir John Meldrum and Major Ireton from Nottingham with some 200 Nottingham horse and foot. Once again, news came of a relief operation being prepared by Newcastle, and so the besieging force broke up and departed, much to Gell's infuriation; he believed that a vital opportunity had been lost to settle accounts with his bitterest local enemy, who 'was brought to great extremety, not able to hold out much longer.' (TA).

AUGUST/SEPTEMBER 1643 — NOTTINGHAM

Having recovered the ground lost to Fairfax in May, Newcastle once more began to turn south and on 6th August reached Lincoln. Nottingham was summoned and the Governor, Sir John Hutchinson prepared for an attack by the Newarkers. It was not long in coming. A Royalist 'fifth column' opened the gates one night and some 600 Newarkers poured in, driving Hutchinson and such of his garrison who had not been taken prisoner in the town, to barricade themselves in the Castle. A plea for help was smuggled out to Gell who promptly sent Molanus at the head of 500 mounted musketeers, to effect a relief.

Sir Richard Byron's cavaliers sacked the town, put Hutchinson's men that were prisoners into some sheep-pens in the market place and then set to work building a fort on Trent bridge — to deny passage and to overawe the Castle — into which they then herded their prisoners and plunder.

Captain White arrived from Leicester with some 400 horse to join Gell's foot and on 28th August they attacked the Newarkers, who stood ready to receive them 'in battalio' in the market place. In the ensuing fight Gell describes how the 500 Parliamentarians charged through the 600 Newarkers, broke them, captured 160 and drove the rest out of the town to seek refuge in their fort on the Trent. This is Gell's version of how the Castle was relieved for the loss of but 5 or 6 horses and one man, a Captain Lieutenant Lenerick, who led Colonel Gell's own troop of horse. One can hardly countenance Sir John's assessment of the casualties — his accounts are notoriously unreliable — nor can we be certain of anything concerning the facts of this engagement. Lucy Hutchinson makes no mention of this considerable success and writes instead:

'Sir John Gell's men, seeing the cavaliers had a mind to be gone, interrupted them not, but being as dexterous at plunder as at fight, they presently went to Toplady's house, who had betrayed the town, and plundered it and some others, while the governor's soldiers were busy clearing the town of the enemy . . . the truth is, Gell's men were nimble youths at that work, yet there was not very much mischief done by them.'

Again, Gell and Mrs. Hutchinson are at variance in their accounts of what followed. Gell states (TR) that some 10 days afterwards, the Nottingham Committee asked him to assist the Nottingham forces in capturing the Trent bridge fort. Sir John says he sent Molanus with between 3 and 4 hundred horse and drove the enemy away. (TA)' . . . our souldiers went againe, and after some tyme we beate the enemie from the bridge, which was of such importance that the governour of the castle professed to Major Mollanus, that unless our souldyers would stay and take the bridge he would quitt the castle, lett the Parliament doe with him what they would.'

He goes on to assert, with some justification, that 'Nottingham town and castle had beene long since in the enemy's possession, had they not had the assistance of Sir John Gell in driving the enemy from them at every tyme of neede . . . ' (TR).

Mrs. Hutchinson on the other hand, tells quite a different tale, and says that immediately after the Newarkers had been driven from the market place and had fled to their fort, her husband the governor entreated the Leicester and Derby men to join with him in an attack upon the bridge fort, before the cavaliers could rally themselves . . . . 'but the major of Derby, an old dull-headed Dutchman, said ten thousand men could not do it and could by no means be entreated to go on, nor to stay one day longer, but to stand by while the governor made the attempt, with his own men.'

She says further that the Derby soldiers would not attempt the fort for lack of ordnance. Hutchinson, upon hearing this, brought out of the Castle two of his guns and bade the Derby men set on, but they refused and stood aside looking on . . 'while he attempted it with his own men; but their Major Molanus, being an old soldier, discouraged our soldiers, and told them it was a vain and impossible attempt . . . '

She says that Molanus came again to Nottingham 'with sixscore foot and dragoons' and repeated his belief that the fort could not be taken. Hutchinson persuaded him and his officers to stay and they went to supper in the Castle, but Gell sent orders for them to return to Derby. As it happened, there was no attack, for during the night, the cavaliers had slipped out of their fortifications, abandoned their works and store of provisions, and safely escaped home to Newark.

Whatever the truth of the matter concerning the battle in the market place and the business of the Trent fort, relations between the two governers became increasingly strained from this time onwards.

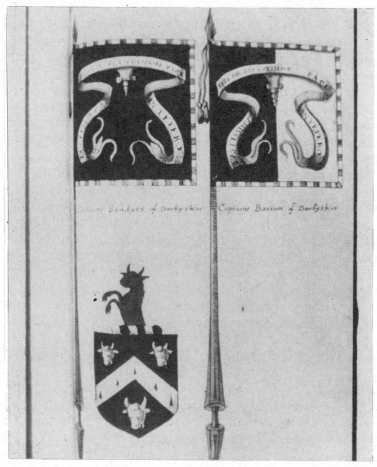

The colours (or cornet) of the Derby Regiment of horse. The motto reads 'Justissimum bellum inquissimae pace antefero' — I hold that peace is sought by a most just war

PART III

NEWCASTLE'S INVASION

OCTOBER 1643 - JANUARY 1644

Meanwhile, the Earl of Newcastle was investing Hull and Fairfax came south in an attempt to raise more forces for his Yorkshire campaign. Gell encouraged Fairfax to come to Derby with his 2,000 horse and tried to enlist his support for another attempt against Tutbury but Sir Thomas was more concerned to find . . 'four or five hundred musquetiers to march with him towards Chesterfield, and from thence to Yorkshire . . ' (TR).

Remarkably, after a few days, Gell agreed to part with 400 foot, to be drawn out of his garrisons in Derbyshire. Remarkable, because Gell knew the local situation and was well aware that Hastings had 2,000 men quartered between Lichfield, Ashby-de-la-Zouch and Tutbury . . . 'still looking for an opportunity to surprise Derby.'

True Relation mentions the fortified places from which these commanded musketeers were to be drawn. There were 100 men at Wingfield Manor, Captain Taylor's company at Wingerworth with 100 men, Captain Stafford's company at Chatsworth, 40 men, and a Captain Hadfield's company whose location and strength is not given. The troops duly marched to Chesterfield under Lieutenant Colonel Gell to meet with Fairfax. The following day they received notice that some 2,000 men of Newcastle's army were about to descend on them and then advance into Derbyshire. Fairfax and his horse turned about and made off in the direction of Nottingham, leaving Gell's men to shift for themselves. They too fled and hastened south to Derby, calling in the garrisons of Chatsworth and Wingerworth as they ran. Gell wrote letters to Fairfax, assuring him that the enemy could be contained if

Fairfax would meet him and join forces, but all he received in return were promises and fair words.

Gell was disgusted and prepared to face Newcastle's second invasion of Derbyshire alone. Members of the Derby Committee were despatched to meet Fairfax at Melton Mowbray and Gell was told that Fairfax would send some forces to assist him at a rendezvous on the Lancashire/Cheshire border. On the strength of this, Gell tells us that he sent Molanus with about 240 horse and dragoons towards Leek, where they stayed for about 2 weeks and engaged some of Newcastle's foraging cavalry with varying success at Hartington and Ashbourne. But overall a bleak time was now at hand for the Roundhead cause in Derbyshire:

'In the meane tyme, the enimy pillaged very neare Derby, and our neighbor countrymen, despaying of any ayd from Sir Thomas Fayrfax, returned home, and so did our horse to us.' (TA).

Fairfax in fact did nothing, and thereafter — as with Hutchinson at Nottingham — Gell long maintained a grievance. Some help arrived in the form of ammunition from London but earnest pleas to Lord Grey for troops fell on deaf ears. Sir John had earlier received a very mixed blessing in the

Thomas Sanders of Little Ireton (1610-1695) and Major of the horse regiment; Gell's severest critic and Derbyshire's most able soldier. Became a colonel in the New Model army during the Cromwellian Protectorate. — Engraving by permission of Derby Local Studies Library.

person of Captain Thomas Sanders, who was re-instated at Derby after an exchange of prisoners, promoted Major by the Earl of Essex and added to the Derby Committee. He was given the task of recruiting a regiment of horse for the Derby garrison, of which Gell himself was to be the titular head as Colonel. Though he and Gell were already bitter personal enemies, Sanders was a competent soldier and did much to ensure that if Newcastle attacked Derby, he would be met with serious resistance.

JANUARY 1644 — DERBY'S DEFENCES

Orders were issued to the areas immediately surrounding the town that the constables should send labourers to Derby to help build up the bulwarks and the earth and timber ramparts. Nothing is known about the nature and extent of these Civil War defences as no plan or map has survived. However, we know that Gell had an artillery train of some 28 pieces commanded by his master of ordnance, Captain German Pole of Radbourne. These weapons, of varying calibres, were mounted on hornworks set about the town according to the directions of one Edward Lion, the garrison engineer. Lion had 20 sappers to assist him, together with a body of townsmen and outside helpers. Odd references in accounts and petitions mention iron reinforced gates at the entries to the town, particularly over the Derwent at St. Mary's Bridge, which was guarded by a drawbridge and possibly an earthwork spur on the north bank. There is also mention of ironwork at the Darand Lane Gates and 'palisadoes' at the spur near St. Peter's Guard. Beyond these tantalising glimpses, nothing more is known of these defences, other than that their creation and maintenance was a great burden on the accounts of the Derby Committee.

DECEMBER 1643 - JANUARY 1644 — DERBY ALONE

As winter approached, Newcastle's troops penetrated throughout the length and breadth of the county and vigorous recruiting began. There was no lack of volunteers and the Commissions of Array brought in some 2,300 men. New regiments were raised for the King's service, towns and country houses were fortified and then on 15th December, the Royalist forces under Sir Francis Mackworth turned on Gell's only surviving garrison outside Derby, Wingfield Manor. It fell only four days later. Three of Gell's officers took this as their signal to desert; Captains Taylor and Clarke made off to Nottingham, followed by Captain Randle Ashenhurst. The latter had commanded Gell's own troop of horse after the death of Captain Lenerick and to Gell's rage, he took 40 troopers with him.

This was the most critical moment of Gell's military career.

He was on his own, cut off from the outside world, seemingly about to be drowned in a flood-tide of Royalist success. Newcastle's Northern Army now linked up with the forces of Lord Loughborough (formerly Henry Hastings, raised to the baronage on 23rd October 1643) and all that Gell had achieved in more than a year of warfare, now seemed washed away.

But though surrounded, the Derby garrison could still bite and according to Sir John, the horse sallied forth against the Royalists at Wingfield, capturing some 40 prisoners. They also met 'the guard of Newcastle at Kilborne' — two miles north of Derby — 'and took one Major Wheeler, with ninety prisoners, all horsed, and their collours: a man paynted and standing with a goold-axe under a greene tree, with this motto: rout and branch.' (TR).

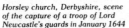

Horsley church, Derbyshire, scene of the capture of a troop of Lord Newcastle's guards in January 1644

The door in the south wall of Horsley church tower, showing musket shot-marks. The Royalist Major Wheeler was captured here, with ninety of his horsemen and their colours

The new year saw Derby still a Parliamentarian island; it also saw on 5th January, Sir John Gell formally commissioned as Governor of the town by the Earl of Essex. It was the high watermark of Gell's power — received during the grimmest moment of the war — but was to lead to all manner of acrimonious political squabbles in Derby, once the military crisis was over.

Major Sanders later argued that Gell's brother, Thomas, and others of his entourage, were plotting to quit Derby and run to Nottingham or Leicester, having safely stored their goods in the houses of known Royalists; but nothing exists to show that Sir John himself was preparing to bolt. Even the taunting letters of his old adversary Lord Loughborough failed to shake his resolve and his correspondence by way of reply is replete with wit and venom. Gell would not be hectored into yielding up the town, nor would he be smooth-talked out of it by the trickery of Sir Simon Every of Egginton.

Sir Simon — a crypto Royalist — posed as a neuter and tried to arrange a parley between the doomed garrison and Newcastle's representatives. It was no more than a thinly disguised attempt to secure the town without the cost of a bloody assault. Gell saw through this pious scheme and rejected Every's spurious embassy as an 'honest broker.' He was wise to do so, for Sir Simon left Derbyshire later in the year and revealed his true colours by serving in the garrisons of Oxford, Lichfield and Tutbury.

Derby remained an island, but the Royalist tide began to recede. The town was never put to the test. Newcastle drew off to face the entry of the Scots into the war and the immediate pressure began to lift. We shall never know whether Gell was bluffing when he wrote of Newcastle;-
' . . . he was sufficiently informed of our resolution to defend itt, and could not be drawne to the enterprise by any means they' — ('our malicious countriemen') — 'could all make to hym. His business in the Northe now calls hym to Yorke . . . ' (TA).

One can only wonder what would have happened if Newcastle or Hastings could have organised themselves more effectively. Would Gell have proved himself a second Massey at Gloucester, or would he have ducked out and run — like his three captains — to Nottingham?

Newcastle's departure did not mean a Royalist abandonment of Derbyshire. Far from it. His houses at Bolsover and at Welbeck over the border in Nottinghamshire, were both strongly held amidst a spider's web of fortified strongpoints straddling the county. Newcastle left six of his Derbyshire colonels behind to hold on to what had been won:-

1. Sir John Frescheville was commissioned to raise further recruits for his regiment of horse and foot to garrison his house at Staveley.

2. Colonel John Milward's regiment of foot and dragoons was settled to defend his home, Snitterton Hall (near Matlock) and to occupy Bakewell.

3. Colonel Rowland Eyre raised a regiment of foot, dragoons and horse to hold his family residence at Hassop Hall and to garrison Chatsworth.

4. Colonel Sir John Fitzherbert had forces of foot and horse at Tissington and Wingfield Manor — the latter place being only nine miles from Derby.

5. The fifth colonel, Sir John Harpur of Swarkestone, was in Lord Loughborough's sphere of influence and quartered his regiment twelve miles from Derby at Burton-on-Trent.

Gell names a sixth colonel left behind by Newcastle to vex him, none other than Sir Simon Every, but — 'having nether men nor armes, and wanting meanes to trouble this country, he went to Oxford to expect the success of the ante-parliament there.' (TR).

There is in fact however, no evidence to suggest that Every actually raised forces for the King. Curiously, Gell omits to mention in this context two further prominent Derbyshire Royalists — Lieutenant Colonel John Shalcross who raised a regiment of horse later in the year, and Colonel Sir Andrew Kniveton of Mercaston who was governor of Tutbury Castle since 1643 and destined to play an important role in Gell's subsequent career.

PART IV

GELL'S COUNTER OFFENSIVE

JANUARY 1644 — BURTON-ON-TRENT

Gell launched his counter-offensive as soon as the 'Northern Popish army' was clear of the county. On 6th January Molanus was sent out to Burton-on-Trent with some horse and dragoons to deal with Harpur's cavaliers. He 'fell upon them, tooke their Major, six captains, eight other officers and five hundred common souldyers, by which act the whole regiment was spoyled.' (TA).

He states that five of the enemy were killed at the storming of the bridge and that Harpur and William Bullock — his Lieutenant Colonel — only managed to escape by running away in the night. We are invited to believe that this prodigious feat was accomplished 'without any loss of our side.' (TR).

Major Sanders took the nascent Derby regiment of horse to Wingfield to harrass the garrison and ambushed there some of Fitzherbert's regiment, taking a number of prisoners, including two un-named captains. He was speedily recalled however, for yet another mission against Burton. It seems that no sooner had Molanus returned to Derby with his captives from Harpur's ruined regiment, than Loughborough himself re-entered the town with his Commissioners of Array. Burton and its bridge over the Trent was essential to him as a means of communication between his 'Flying Army' based at Ashby and the Royalist garrisons at Tutbury Castle and throughout Derbyshire.

Sanders arrived with 400 horse, rushed the town so successfully that he took many prisoners and only narrowly missed taking Lord Loughborough himself.

FEBRUARY 1644 — KINGS MILLS

Beaten out of Burton, Loughborough reinforced his garrison at Kings Mills on the banks of the Trent near Castle Donington. Gell himself led out almost the entire garrison of horse, foot and artillery on 5th February, determined that Loughborough should not have a safe passage over the Trent.

The stone house was well fortified with works and trenches and Gell's cannon made little impression. So, during the night, a forlorn hope of 30 picked men scaled the works, 'beat down the windows and stormed in and so forced them to cry quarter.'

Twenty of Gell's men were wounded and five killed in the attack which Gell reported to the Earl of Essex as . . . 'as desperate a piece of service as any such petty business hath been in the North.' The captured numbered two hundred, including a captain, a lieutenant and fifty soldiers, together with 'some malignant countrymen fledd thyther for safetie.' (TA).

FEBRUARY 1644 — ASHBOURNE

Control of a vital bridge was the issue which occasioned the next operation to be undertaken by the Derby garrison. The bridge at Ashbourne governed the movement in and out of Staffordshire and was the main route to Manchester. Royalist forces began to congregate at Ashbourne and 'kept off the countrey people from the markett.' (TR).

But the Staffordshire Parliamentarians feared that this gathering of cavaliers presaged an attempt by Hastings to raise the siege of Biddulph House near Leek. Accordingly, Gell despatched Major Sanders to Ashbourne with 500 horse and dragoons to break up any intended relief operation.

Sanders quartered his men at Ashbourne, but hearing that the Royalists hoped to surprise him, he lined the lanes and hedges with dragoons and attacked the would-be attackers in the rear with the horse regiment. The Royalists were completely routed and fled to Tissington, losing some 170 men prisoners.

'Their officers all runne away cowardly, so that the greatest officer wee tooke was but a cornet.' (TA).

NORTH MIDLAND GARRISONS — SPRING 1644

1. Staveley 2. Chatsworth 3. Biddulph 4. Tissington 5. Wingfield
6. Thurgarton 7. Shelford 8. Wiverton 9. Wilne Ferry 10. King's Mills
11. Lapley 12. Burleigh (Leics.) 13. Chillington 14. Rushall 15. Patshull
16. Wrottesley

a. Eccleshall b. Tamworth c. Bagworth d. Burleigh (Rutland)

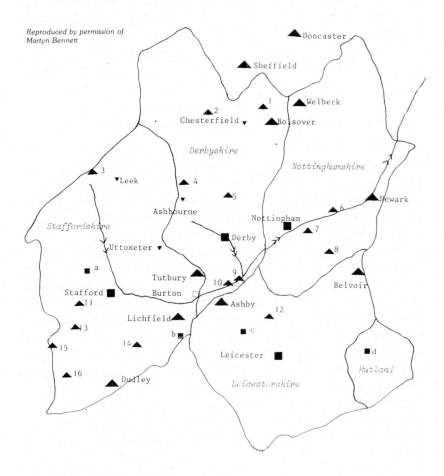

Reproduced by permission of Martyn Bennett

▼ Possible Royalist Garrison

▢ Unoccupied Town

▲ Royalist Garrisons (Major)

▲ Royalist Garrisons (Minor)

■ Parliamentarian Garisons (Major)

■ Parliamentarian Garisons (Minor)

⤜⟩⟩ River

─────── County Boundary

Derbyshire: County Name

The Royalist strongholds now faced ever increasing pressure from the Derby garrison and in particular, from its new regiment of horse. Constant fights took place between rival patrols as each side sought mastery over the countryside on which to levy contributions. Gell's narrative emphasises the difficulty of recording every single action in this small-scale localised war of ambush and sudden raid:-

'It is impossible to relate our continual and almost daylie incounters with the Earle of Newcastle's garrisons . . . ' (TA).

17-29 MARCH 1644
RUPERT'S RELIEF OF NEWARK

However, a bigger operation was in the offing as the Spring approached. The Derbyshire strongpoints were, after all, but satellite garrisons of the major Royalist base at Newark and it was against this hornet's nest that Sir John Meldrum was commanded to lead the joint Parliamentary forces of Lincolnshire, Leicestershire, Nottinghamshire and Derby.

Major Sanders and 500 Derby horse and dragoons made a rendezvous with Meldrum's army at Nottingham on 24th February. The total strength of the Roundhead force was in the region of some 2,000 horse and 5,000 foot, with 11 pieces of artillery. On the 29th it moved against Newark and a powerful siege commenced. Prolonged resistance could not be expected and strenuous efforts were made by the Royalists outside Newark to mount a relief and lift the siege. Foremost amongst them was Colonel Frescheville, who wrote to Loughborough telling him that the Derbyshire horse regiments were mustering again at Ashbourne and suggesting that Prince Rupert himself be informed of the dangerous situation at Newark.

Gell at Derby, knew well enough what was afoot, but with his cavalry away serving at Newark, he could do nothing to impede the Royalist concentrations in the north of the county. But far more worrying was the news that Rupert had marched from Chester and reached Lichfield on March 17th, with the object of linking up with Loughborough's 'Flying Army' of 2,700 men at Ashby.

As in the previous Winter when Newcastle's army had descended on Derbyshire from the North, Gell wrote frantically for assistance to Fairfax and to the Committee of Both Kingdoms requesting help from neighbouring counties, but met the same success as before. Nothing could be done to help.

The Derbyshire Royalist regiments of Frescheville, Eyre and Harpur joined Prince Rupert's 4,500 men at Ashby on the 18th, despite a bungled attempt by Meldrum's cavalry commander, Sir Edward Hartop, to intercept and prevent their union.

On 21st March, Rupert's augmented army reached Newark and the battle to save the place began. Muskham bridge and the area to the West of Newark Castle — called the Island — were held by some Lincoln and Nottinghamshire foot, plus the bulk of the Derby horse, commanded by Major Molanus. Here they were attacked on Rupert's arrival by a sudden sally made by the Newarkers under Sir Richard Byron. The Derby horse broke and fled and Molanus himself abandoned the foot and made off. Meanwhile, Rupert's cavalry smashed into the rest of Meldrum's horse and the Roundheads — including the remainder of the Derby horse and dragoons — were driven into the area known as the Spittal and compelled to surrender. In this significant action, the largest in which Derby forces had so far participated, Gell lost:-

'about two hundred horse and dragoons, with their arms, and the men all stript to their very skin, contrary to the articles of agreement.' (TR).

The agreement he refers to, was that by which Meldrum was allowed to march away with drums, colours, horses, swords, baggage and personal belongings; but had to abandon his 11 cannon, ammunition and 3,000 muskets to the victorious Royalists. Presumably the losses bemoaned by Gell concerned only arms and equipment and possibly horses rather than men, for Meldrum's casualties numbered no more than 200 in all. These deficiencies were soon made good once the troopers returned to Derby, for just over a week later the whole force of horse and dragoons was once again in action and behaved in such a creditable way as to redeem its tarnished reputation.

Newark had been an unpleasant experience — worse than that under Ballard in February 1643 — but the Derby forces had not yet seen the last of the place. They were destined to serve there again on at least three occasions, as we shall see, before the town finally surrendered on 8th May 1646.

31 MARCH 1644 — FIGHT AT EGGINTON HEATH

Rupert's army then returned to Ashby on 29th and remained there for three days further. Gell was deeply concerned for the safety of Derby, knowing that Lord Loughborough and the Derbyshire contingent in the Royal army would be badgering the Prince to make an attempt against the town and resettle old scores with its governor. But Rupert was conscious that Loughborough's army was basically a hotch-potch of forces temporarily drawn out from various local garrisons, to which they now needed to return.

Two of these horse contingents — totalling some 600 men — left Ashby on the 31st and set off to return to their respective quarters. One was Colonel Sir Andrew Kniveton's party from Tutbury Castle and the other Sir John Frescheville's — doubtless returning to the Ashbourne area from which it was mustered to assist in the Newark campaign.

These two 'regiments' — more probably an amalgam of Derbyshire garrison troops — marched through Repton and Willington — 'towns very malignant,' crossed the Trent and reached Egginton Heath, only four miles from Tutbury on the Staffs. border. Here they were confronted by a body of the Derby horse. What followed was the largest skirmish in the field and the nearest thing to a battle that occurred in Derbyshire during the entire Civil War.

There seems to be no Royalist version recounting what befell and we are very much at the mercy of Gell's account in his 'True Relation' and on the Parliamentary news report reproduced in the Thomason Tracts (TT); though both are fortunately supplemented by observations later made by Major Sanders.

Sir John relates that the 'entire' horse regiment (some 350 strong) was sent out on his orders to intercept the Royalists who were 'plundering some towns about Egginton'. Upon learning of the strength of the enemy, Gell tells us that he then despatched Major Molanus with a further 400 foot 'to lye in the lanes wayting, lest his horse should bee forced to retreate, that they might be ready to fall uppon the enemy if they should pursue them.'

The account in TT however, though almost certainly composed by Gell himself immediately after the action, says that a reinforcement of horse was sent out from Derby to bring the regiment's strength up to 400 and wholly omits any mention of the foot.

Major Sanders, writing a year or so after the event, relates that on the night before the encounter, he ordered out a party of 100 horse under his trusted friend Captain Nathaniel Barton and . . 'gave him an order that he should have an eye upon the fords at Twyford and Willington, which was done accordingly.'

Sanders was clearly anticipating some kind of Royalist activity and was taking pains to secure the vital Trent crossings. Having issued his orders, Sanders remained all day in Derby at the house of Captain Robert Mellor — an officer in Gell's foot regiment and the son of Derby's first mayor — when news suddenly arrived that 'the horse were engaged in the lane near Egginton Heath.' He sounded the alarm and ordered every man to mount and to ride to Barton's rescue. However, his troop had already set out and was patrolling towards Sanders's own country house at Lullington, some 8 miles to the south of Egginton. Sanders found the stables locked and being unable to get his horse, he ran back to Captain Mellor — 'to borrow one of his, but they were all gone forth. Being thus disappointed, I marched out with Major Molanus and Captain Mellor and the foot but before we got half a mile from the town, news came that all was done and the enemy beaten.' He adds significantly, 'All the while I never saw the Colonel nor received any order from him.'

Gell's account agrees that the foot saw no action and says that the Derby horse charged the Royalists and scattered them. Many of the fugitives were driven into the Trent where

Looking east along the river Trent from Newton Solney towards Repton, the spot where Royalist cavalry were allegedly driven into the water after their rout on Egginton Heath 31st March 1644

they drowned and a total of some 200 prisoners were taken. The rest were chased off as far as Repton on the road back to Ashby.

The TT account has more detail of the fight and again lists the terrible losses sustained by Frescheville's men. These can be largely discounted as further evidence of Gell's unreliability and bias in the matter of casualties, particularly as the Roundheads suffered no losses whatever. Further, the account mentions a number of Royalist officers killed and wounded:

Major (Thomas) Bates — (killed) of Sir John Harpur's regiment; he was in fact alive in 1654.

Major (Gilbert) Kniveton — (wounded) brother of Sir Andrew Kniveton the governor of Tutbury Castle and a particular enemy of Gell's since the very start of the war.

Captain Arthur Lowe — (drowned) of Colonel Fitzherbert's regiment, in which he and at least 3 of his brothers served. Arthur did not in fact drown and lived to claim as an Indigent Officer in 1663.

That the Derbyshire Royalist horse suffered a serious defeat only a week after its triumphs before Newark, cannot be doubted, but we may confidently reject the casulaty figures as propaganda invented by Gell to inflate his reputation in London. No wonder that Mrs. Hutchinson sneeringly remarked that Gell 'kept the journalists in pension' whereby 'he indirectly purchased a name in history, which he never merited.'

There remain a number of perplexing issues surrounding this enagagement which the sources — though admittedly inadequate — fail to explain. For example, if Gell's horse had been roughly handled at the battle of Newark and lost some 200 men including their arms and equipment, how is it that barely a week later, they were able to take on and defeat a force of Royalist cavalry about a third stronger in numbers and yet suffer no casualties themselves in the process? and all this was the work of a Captain Rhodes — an officer of no appreciable previous experience; in fact hitherto unknown. Yet Gell specifically mentions him in TR:

'Captayne Rhoades being chief commander thereof.' Perhaps part of an explanation may lie in the fact that Rhodes was the only officer in the horse regiment who later remained loyal to Gell and who stood out in opposition to the rest, who were supporters of Major Sanders. Interestingly, Gell says nothing of Captain Barton, who presumably first encountered the Royalists as they forded the Trent in the Twyford/ Willington area and conducted a holding defence whilst drawing back and getting news to Derby. It may also be significant that Gell's account published in London in TT shortly after the battle, does not mention the name of the Parliamentarian commander. Yet the 'True Account' published after the war, gives Rhodes a deliberate mention.

One may conclude from all this that TR retrospectively reflects local political conflicts which came to a head once the Civil War was over. Indeed, as we shall see, Gell later credits Rhodes with military achievements during the fighting around Tutbury that more reliably belonged to others. As he was wont to puff up his own successes, so too was he prepared to do on behalf of his cronies. But this is speculation. We shall never know the name of the real victor of Egginton Heath; it may in truth have been Captain Rhodes as Gell says, or Captain Barton — who after all, was the man on the spot. Though Barton of course, as a close friend of Sanders, would be unlikely to claim merit in any account penned by Sir John Gell.

It is only the existence of the Sanders manuscript itself that obliges us to reject as candidates for this honour, Major Molanus and Major Sanders.

There is a final postscript to this business in the discovery of a 'cavalier' sword at the end of the 19th century in the thatched roof of a cottage in Egginton village. The sword dates from the time of the Civil War and was presumably secreted there by one of the fleeing Royalist officers.

APRIL 1644

Molanus and 500 horse and dragoons were sent to Leicester to await the arrival of a convoy of some 40 pieces of ordnance coming from London to Derby via Peterborough. A Royalist attempt at interception, Gell tells us, was frustrated by Molanus pausing for 4 days at Tamworth. Molanus then marched to rendezvous with the convoy at Peterborough. Such a strong guard was needed in order to deter attacks from Ashby and Newark. The scouts were vigilant and no further Royalist sorties were made. The guns and ammunition safely reached Derby. Gell later accused Major Sanders of disobeying an order to command the horse in person during the Peterborough expedition. The Major maintained that he was given no such order. He states that the captains of horse all supported his view that the entire regiment should undertake the escort duty but that overall command should be exercised by Major Molanus, as the latter knew more about artillery and would therefore be more competent in taking care of the guns.

PART V

MARSTON MOOR . . .
. . . THE TIDE TURNS

MAY, JUNE, JULY 1644 — MARSTON MOOR

When the troopers returned, orders came from Parliament to send forces to assist in the campaign being waged in Yorkshire. Newcastle's army was besieged at York and Prince Rupert was on his way with a relieving army. A Parliamentarian army began to gather under the Earl of Denbigh to head Rupert off and Gell contributed 300 horse and dragoons under Captain Rhodes. Earlier, Denbigh had requested that Gell send him 500 horse and 500 foot to oppose the Prince in Lancashire, but the boot was now on the other foot and Gell could reply somewhat drily:

'I am well assured your Lordship doth not require the quitting of our garrison, being the key to the north and the frontier garrison . . . There are 2,000 of the Marquis of Newcastle's horse within ten miles of Derby besides ten garrisons of the enemy in the county and near its confines . . . This is the real truth.'

Denbigh's efforts were indeed dilatory and even when he had managed to muster a very respectable army of 12,000, he still did nothing to impede Rupert's march across Lancashire and up to the gates of York.

Rupert himself had meanwhile summoned Royalist garrisons once more to issue out and join his field army. As before, the Derbyshire Royalists reduced their strongpoints to skeleton strength, abandoned Chatsworth garrison and under Colonel Frescheville, the Derbyshire contingent marched out at the beginning of June and joined the Prince's army in Cheshire. Gell's intelligence estimated their strength at around

300 horse, 30 dragoons and 220 foot, under Colonels Frescheville, Eyre and Milward. They participated in the disastrous battle of Marston Moor on 2nd July — the horse formed part of Sir Charles Lucas's brigade under General Goring on the left wing whilst the foot formed a separate body in the second line of Tillier's foot. It is likely that many perished in the battle, particularly amongst the foot soldiers.

The survivors trailed back into Derbyshire, shocked and demoralised, and took refuge in their garrisons at Staveley, Bolsover and Wingfield. Some, like Colonel John Milward — who had commanded the Derbyshire foot at Marston Moor — thought the writing was on the wall and sought to make their peace with Parliament by compounding for their estates.

18 JULY 1644 — WILNE FERRY

Gell's horse and dragoons now returned from the north; Newcastle's once formidable power was now broken and the tide was on the turn. Sir John was able to co-operate with Lord Grey for a joint attack on Wilne Ferry, where Loughborough had built a strong fort and garrisoned it with 300 men 'for hindering the passage over the Trent.' (TR). It must be remembered that this was then an important routeway for trade — particularly lead — which was brought on horses from Wirksworth for storage at Derby, before being carried in carts and waggons to Wilne Ferry, five miles distant. From here it was embarked in barges and carried down the Trent to Gainsborough and Hull for shipment to London and overseas. Gell had extensive interests in the lead trade and one may perhaps see in the attack on Wilne, something of a happy conjunction of private financial interest and military necessity!

This was Loughborough's second attempt to gain a foothold on the Trent and was dealt with as swiftly and successfully as was his earlier endeavour with the fort at Kings Mills in February. Gell simply set up his greatly augmented artillery and made ready to storm the fort, whereupon the defenders cried out for quarter. Other sources however, describe events in more detail and inform us that some 60 or so cartloads of

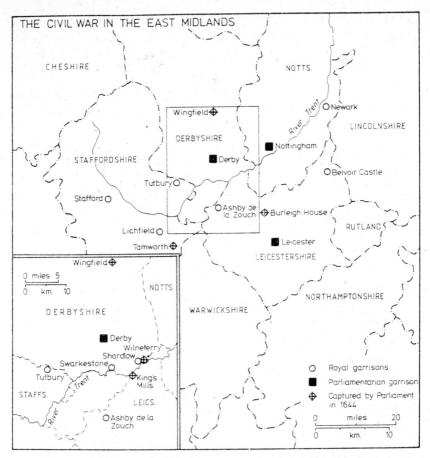

THE CIVIL WAR IN THE EAST MIDLANDS

The Civil War in the East Midlands — map reproduced thanks to Martyn Bennett

hay were pushed towards the Royalist works and then set on fire. The resulting smoke blinded and scorched the defenders so that they surrendered to a man. Thereafter, Gell was able to move his horse and dragoons closer to Ashby, to harass and encircle Loughborough's men — so that "they durst noe more sturr to robb carriers.' (TR).

28 JULY 1644 — WINGFIELD MANOR

The time had come for a final push against the remaining Royalist garrisons, depleted and demoralised by the news of Marston Moor and Gell undertook to assist his old rival and fellow governor — Colonel Hutchinson of Nottingham — in a joint attack on Wingfield Manor, 'because it was as great an annoyance to Nottinghamshire as it was to Derbyshire.' (TR).

Gell's troops now ranged out from Derby and re-entered Chesterfield in the north, harrying the Royalist gentry round about, pillaging and raiding. Frescheville wrote angrily to Gell from his house at Staveley on 10th July, accusing his men of 'cruel outrages upon the persons of harmless people which never bore arms, as the mortal wounding of my keeper and the murdering of a stranger that came by chance to his house. They have likewise taken the minister of Staveley, a man in life and teaching without blame and a tenant of mine, one Peter Briggs.'

The tables were turned and Gell meant to exploit the new situation. He mustered all his forces and marched out to Wingfield, leaving only 2 companies of foot at Derby. In ten days time he was met by the Nottingham forces and the garrison was invested by something like 1,000 foot and 2,000 horse.

Loughborough now stirred himself to retaliate. The plan was to use the garrisons of Lichfield and Tutbury in a co-ordinated relief operation. Accordingly he wrote on 30th July to Colonel Bagot, governor of Lichfield, telling him to assemble his men at Burton-on-Trent where Loughborough himself intended to join them with a force from Ashby. Meanwhile Colonel Rowland Eyre was instructed to march from Hassop with his regiment and link up with the rest of the forces mustering at Burton.

Somehow Sanders got wind of the scheme and drew off from the siege all the horse and dragoons. He pounced on Eyre's hapless regiment en route whilst it spent the night in Boylestone church — presumably without a guard — for every man was taken without loss to the attackers. The dragoons were left behind to guard captives in the church whilst Major Sanders led the horse on to Burton and, 'after two or three hot encounters' (TR) he forced Colonel Bagot's men out of the town and back to Lichfield.

This nicely judged little operation was a serious set-back for

Colonel Rowland Eyre of Hassop (1600-1674) whose regiment of horse spent the night in Boylestone church en route to Burton-on-Trent in August 1644 and was captured there by Sanders and the Derby horse

The south chancel door at Boylestone, out through which Eyre's two hundred men filed, to be disarmed and marched as prisoners to Derby

Loughborough, and, as we shall see, for the long term continuance of his Derbyshire garrisons.

Gell estimated that for the loss of only 5 men killed, Sanders had killed 17 of the enemy and taken a total of 300 prisoners, including Eyre's men captured at Boylestone. The whole lot were marched back to Derby under escort, leaving the triumphant Sanders to return with the horse to Wingfield Manor — having accomplished a thorough ruination of Lord Loughborough's scheme to relieve the strongest of the Derbyshire garrisons.

The Derby regiment of horse had again proved its worth and performed valiantly but the work afoot at Wingfield was of an altogether different order, being the slow and grim business of tackling a determined and well-entrenched adversary and it dragged on into August. The governor, Colonel Roger Molyneux, was resolved to hold out for as long as he could. The walls were strong and Gell's ordnance could accomplish little; the garrison of some 300 men had ample provisions and were in good heart. Twice at least they sallied out and captured parties of the besiegers. Attempts to cut off the water supply were answered by Molyneux sinking a well; then Gell tried mining but the garrison foiled him with a counter-mine. Sir John was forced to the conclusion that without other means, the stronghold could not be taken unless the garrison could be 'pined out.' But this would take time and money and both were in short supply. Besides, Gell was anxious to prosecute the war more vigorously against the Marston Moor survivors and being tied down to a lengthy siege was the last thing he wanted.

Having reached an impasse, Gell then heard that the Earl of Manchester's army was marching south from the victory at York and had reached Doncaster on the 26th July. However, he had to wait for help while Manchester divided his army and turned first against Welbeck in Nottinghamshire and then against Sheffield Castle. The former — Newcastle's own property — fell at the first summons and a garrison of Nottinghamshire foot was immediately installed.

Meanwhile, Manchester's second in command — the Scot, Major-General Crawford, with 1200 foot and 3 large cannon — settled down before Sheffield Castle and on 7th August began to batter the fortifications. A great gun called 'The Queen's Pocket Pistol' had arrived and it soon effected a breach. Crawford was now ready to storm the castle. The governor, Colonel Beaumont, saw that the game was up and after a last summons, surrendered the place on 10th August.

The entry into Derbyshire was thus forced open, sounding the death knell for the fortified houses of north Derbyshire: Staveley, Bolsover and Wingfield. They were no match for the monsters of ordnance that Crawford now threatened to bring against them.

Staveley was the first intended victim, but its owner, Colonel Frescheville had cunningly secured a letter of protection from Lord Fairfax at York. The facts are not clear, but it would seem that he was captured at Marston Moor (or York when it surrendered shortly after) and had given his parole not to fight against the Parliament in exchange for his liberty. Gell was outraged, for here was his old enemy and the virtual leader of the northern Derbyshire Royalists — whose house still held a garrison of 200 musketeers and 12 guns — yet protected from retribution and vengeance by order of a Yorkshireman!

Gell wrote on 7th August to Sir Thomas Fairfax protesting that such protection must have been granted due to a misunderstanding, for Frescheville 'was both the first and most active of our countrymen that ever took up arms against Parliament and he is not yet willing to lay them down.' Gell begged Sir Thomas to recant his protection so that his antagonist 'must submit to the mercy of Parliament's forces,' which meant in effect, submission to Gell himself. But on this occasion Sir John was to be baulked of his prey. Fairfax replied that he had not been misinformed; Frescheville had laid down his commission and sworn that he would yield himself and his house to Fairfax whenever he might be called upon to do so. That requirement was made on 12th August and promptly complied with. Frescheville had had enough.

Though but little of the original house now survives, it is immediately apparent that such a structure would have had no chance against 'The Queen's Pocket Pistol' and its awesome fellows. So, to Gell's chagrin, one of his chief opponents succeeded in avoiding summary military justice meted out by Sir John Gell's troops. Staveley's garrison, however, escaped to Newark, to be joined there on the 14th by that of Bolsover.

Major Muschamp, the governor of Newcastle's great house at Bolsover, commanded a place of great natural strength which was furnished with everything necessary for a siege, except provisions! Because of this fatal omission, he quietly yielded before Crawford's battery could be put in position.

Thus two of Derbyshire's Royalist garrisons peacefully rendered themselves up, but the third — at Wingfield — continued to defy its besiegers.

The water supply began to dwindle and on 12th August, Molyneux issued special orders regarding the amounts to be issued to members of the garrison. The list mentions a number of officers then serving in the garrison and contains mention of Captains John and Arthur Lowe and a major Thomas Eyre, who were Derbyshire officers in the Marquis of Newcastle's army. They and most of the seven others named in the

~ WINGFIELD MANOR ~

document were refugees from Marston Moor. But Wingfield was a far from ideal refuge, for on 15th August, Gell's importunings bore fruit and Crawford arrived to survey the Manor's defences. Two days later his troops and artillery arrived and took up quarters around Alfreton, the nearest town. It took but two days more for his great guns to join those of Gell and commence the fearful bombardment. After three hours the 32lb. balls had effected a breach and Molyneux — or his successor — sent out Major Eyre to arrange a parley.

Crawford demanded surrender but Eyre asked if he might send word to Bolsover and Sheffield to see how they fared. He refused to believe that they had already fallen, even when shown the articles of their surrender. Realising that time was wasting, Crawford recommenced the battering and soon enlarged the breach. A storming was forestalled by the governor's drums beating for another parley, which could have no other outcome but surrender. So, on 20th August, Derbyshire's last Royalist garrison gave up the struggle, being free to march to Lichfield or such places as they desired 'without plundering, pillaging, or any let or molestation whatsoever.'

Of the 220 men who marched out, some 40 officers and men were allowed to proceed to the nearest remaining local Royalist garrison at Tutbury Castle; the rest returned to their homes under protection from the Earl of Manchester.

This triumph, though largely the work of Major-General Crawford, gained Gell further plaudits in London. The former rejoined Manchester's army at Lincoln, leaving Gell master of the field. The only sour note was the installation of a Nottinghamshire garrison — to be paid for by Derbyshire — under the command of Colonel Randle Ashenhurst, one of Gell's former foot regiment officers who had deserted the Derby garrison during the crisis of December, 1643. His appointment as governor of Bolsover — and the fact that the costs of it were to be met by Derbyshire contributions — must have rankled with Sir John sorely. Yet this notwithstanding, Gell's Royalist enemies in the county were broken and cowed; a few still defied him — those who had fled to the garrisons of Tutbury and Newark — but matters had never yet stood so favourably disposed. Now vengeance could be exacted and Gell set about the business of sequestrating the estates of his foes. Now was the time to pay soldiers and to line pockets!

NOVEMBER 1644
MINOR GARRISONS : BARTON / COLEORTON

Gell's principal antagonists were concentrated at Tutbury Castle but with Crawford's departure, he had insufficient men and material for a full scale attack. The next best thing was to bottle up the defenders by placing a force of observation close by, that could issue out the moment Kniveton's men made a sortie. This was duly done at Barton Blount and a detachment of the horse regiment was permanently stationed there. This new fortification at Barton had a deleterious effect on the Castle's garrison; it could no longer set out to range over the surrounding countryside gathering contributions from the populace and as Sir John put it '(we) soe kept Tutbury men in, that they could do noe hurt to Derbyshire.' (TR).

To tighten the noose still further, Gell sought to put some of his men into Burton-on-Trent but the Staffordshire Committee objected, alleging that the town was too impoverished after being fought over by both sides for the past two years to be able to sustain and pay a regular garrison. A Staffordshire force was temporarily quartered there in place of Gell's greycoats.

Gell then assisted the Leicestershire Parliamentarians to deal with the menace of Ashby in a similar manner and throughout November all the horse and dragoons he could spare were helping to establish a watching garrison at Coleorton, just three miles distant from Loughborough's headquarters.

NOVEMBER — REVENGE DEFERRED

Ironically, the clearing of Derbyshire marked the high water mark of Gell's personal authority. Hitherto, the Derbyshire Committee had submitted to Gell in order that the county might be rid of 'malignants.' The exigencies of the military situation demanded support for the governor, but once this object was attained, Gell's high-handed and arbitrary rule would no longer pass unchallenged. Though this work is intended to delineate the purely military events within and around the county, some brief mention must be made of the county Committee which from the winter of 1644 began to exert an increasing pressure against the governor of Derby's personal rule. This was not wholly due to the overthrow of internal dangers presented by the Royalists. The Committee's emergence from abject docility was occasioned by a crucial change in its membership; originally composed of Gell's relations, family friends and hangers-on, the appointment of Thomas Sanders in October, 1643, by order of Parliament and his promotion to Major by the Earl of Essex's commission, put a foot in the door for that growing party in Derby who opposed Sir John on the grounds of religion, morality, politics and the future conduct of the war.

Furthermore, the Committee of both Kingdoms now sought to use Sir John's horse and foot regiments further afield, at the very time when he purposed to use them against his last remaining recalcitrant enemies ensconced in Tutbury and Ashby. These he had fought against on and off during the past two years but time and time again had been distracted from administering the coup de grace by extraneous events. Now, when the time of reckoning was at hand, the Derby Committee began to resist his authority and the Committee of Both Kingdoms (CBK) ordered the Derby forces on service beyond the county boundaries. Small wonder that Gell herefrom, becomes increasingly quarrelsome and vindictive. This, together with Parliament's failure to re-imburse him in full for what he alleged to have laid out in support of the cause, explains in some measure his deepening disillusionment with the war and his apparent reluctance to prosecute it with his former accustomed vigour.

CHESTER AND NEWARK 1644

Sir John's fond hope of a speedy settlement of affairs with Sir Andrew Kniveton, governor of Tutbury Castle, was dashed when the CBK ordered six troops of the Derby horse and dragoons to assist Sir William Brereton at the siege of Chester, where they remained till April of the following year.

A further brake on Gell's ambitions was provided by the insistence of the CBK and Fairfax that Bolsover, Chatsworth and Hardwick House should be garrisoned and dismissed Gell's pleas that they should be slighted in order to save him an unwelcome expenditure in men and money.

During the winter of 1644, Major Sanders appears to have served briefly with the contingent of Derby horse assisting Sir William Brereton in Cheshire, for Sir William thereafter showed a warm regard for him. It may be that Sanders — as a 'godly man' — and zealous Puritan, was also attracted to Brereton and may well have wished to defect and become one of Brereton's officers. The experience of serving amongst other forces with different officers, with better conditions of service and pay, perhaps encouraged capable men to consider transferring their loyalties from the domineering Gell to commanders of more equable temper.

The Derby horse served as 'auxiliaries' in the leaguer

around Chester and in December are mentioned as a constituent part of Brereton's army besieging Beeston Castle, a satellite garrison of Royalist Chester. They were also present at the battle of Denbigh in November and were noted as making a significant contribution to the Roundhead victory.

OCTOBER 1644 — VALE OF BELVOIR

Meanwhile, the requirement to deal with Newark became more urgent as the Newarkers stepped up their ever deeper raids into Lincolnshire and Derbyshire. Fairfax's forces were sent to Lincoln and Colonel Fleetwood's to Stamford in preparation for a decisive siege. The remaining six troops of the Derby horse, plus the Nottingham horse, met with Fairfax and joined Colonel Rossiter and his Lincoln horse in the Vale of Belvoir. The governor of Newark, Sir John Byron, did his best to attack the engulfing concentration of enemy cavalry but at a sizeable skirmish at Denton (between Grantham and Belvoir) he came up against Colonel Rossiter and the combined Parliamentarian cavalry. He was routed completely and driven back behind his fortifications. Gell graphically describes that Byron 'had much a doe to save himself, in running on ffoot to Belvoyer Castle, leaving his perriwicke behind him on the ground, many of them taken prisoners, and our troopes brought with them about thirty good horse to Derby, which made some satisfaction for our losse before Newarke,' (in March 1643). (TR).

JANUARY 1645 — SANDERS v GELL

It was probably about this time that matters came to a head between Gell and Major Sanders. The latter — who had presumably returned from service in Cheshire and taken part in the successful manoeuvre against Byron — suddenly refused to obey Gell's command to return again to what one might term, the 'Newark front.' A letter preserved in the Gresley papers informs us that the CBK commanded Gell to send his horse once more to join with Fairfax for the purpose of blocking up Newark on the north side. Sanders refused to take command of them saying he had to go to London on private business. Upon his return, he was again ordered to join the horse about Newark but refused, so Gell had him arrested for insubordination and confined him to his house pending an appeal to Essex for further instructions. Sanders then compiled a written reply to Gell's allegations of misconduct and argued that he had gone to London on a matter of public business which was known to Gell and all other members of the Committee. Upon his return, he confirmed that he was ordered to join the regiment, then quartered at Southwell, but was ill and could not go immediately and so Gell had him confined for about two weeks until a letter arrived from the Earl of Essex ordering Sanders's release and the dropping of all charges against him.

FEBRUARY, MARCH, APRIL 1645 — CHESHIRE

Although the Roundheads now closely invested Newark and had high hopes of the town's surrender, something of a Royalist renaissance occurred and showed that though Derbyshire had been cleared, the King's men raised from the county earlier in the war, were far from beaten.

Sir Marmaduke Langdale advanced to relieve Newark and at Melton Mowbray on 25th February, inflicted a sharp reverse on Rossiter's Lincoln horse in revenge for Denton. Meanwhile a party of some 500 cavalry from Newark under Colonel Molyneux, broke through the encircling Parliamentarians and penetrated deep into Derbyshire as far as Wirksworth. They fell upon the Derby Committee and its escort of 120 horse and took the lot prisoner back to Newark.

Further west, Prince Maurice relieved Brereton's siege of Chester and compelled him to fall back to Nantwich, where he remained until the Prince departed on the 13th of March.

The six troops of Derby horse and dragoons were serving as part of Brereton's army when they were peremptorily recalled to Derby by Gell. Brereton valued their assistance and was much annoyed by Gell's interference. The latter, however, excused himself by stating that Hutchinson urgently required succour against a raid by the Newarkers, who, under their new governor, Sir Richard Willis, had launched a surprise attack on Nottingham bridge. But there is more to this affair than Gell's bland statement in TR that he was obliged to remove the six troops in order to assist his fellow governor at Nottingham.

Correspondence contained in Brereton's Letter Books reveals a number of references to the Derby forces between 13th March and 16th April. We learn that Gell was behind a number of machinations to get his cavalry back from Brereton's clutches; the six captains — Joseph Swettenham, Nathaniel Barton, Robert Hope, Samuel Sleigh, Thomas Watson and John Goring — wrote to Brereton complaining that Gell was denying them their pay. It appears that Sir John had ordered the collectors of Scarsdale Hundred to divert the money levied, to pay his 'loyal' captains of horse, Rhodes and Frith, and to give them preferential treatment. The outraged six averred that Gell had earlier promised to ensure that they should be paid first.

Gell had indicated to Captain Hope's troop that he would pay them only if they returned at once to Derby. Accordingly, some thirty of them deserted their colours and were on the road to Derby crying 'Horse and away to Derby!' when Captain Hope overtook them and managed to persuade them to return to their duty. Being largely raised by Major Sanders and considered to be his creatures, Gell had sought to deprive them of their pay as means of forcing them to return to Derby and to his obedience.

The embarrassed officers, seeing their disgruntled troopers unpaid and unwilling to continue in Cheshire, besought Brereton for assistance, 'lest after much cost and hard service (we) become a ridicule to our foes'.

At least one troop — that of a Captain Villiers — had already gone back to Derby and so to avoid an unseemly exodus from Brereton's army, the officers petitioned to be granted an honourable discharge. Brereton had no means at his disposal to pay his Derby auxiliaries and so had unwillingly to accept their withdrawal to Derby as a fait accompli. The officers indicated that they themselves would have preferred to continue in his service and Brereton's own letters certainly reveal that he entertained a warm personal regard for the Derby captains and continually hoped for their return. This however, did not come about until the Autumn of 1645 when Major Sanders and a detachment of the Derby horse returned to the siege of Chester, at a time when Gell's influence was decidedly on the wane for reasons connected with his behaviour during the Naseby campaign. But in April, Gell was able to outface Brereton and get his way. He reported to the CBK that there were more pressing duties for his horse regiment close at hand against the Newarkers and that in any event, his troopers would need pay and clothing before they could venture once more as far as Chester.

PART VI

THE KING'S LAST CHANCE

MAY, JUNE 1645 — THE NASEBY CAMPAIGN

These deliberations were cut short by the King's sudden move from Oxford on May 7th. His intentions and destination remained a mystery to the CBK, so local commanders were sent the following instructions:

'We have written to Lord Fairfax for 200 Yorkshire horse, to Sir John Gell for 500 of the Derbyshire horse and have commissioned him, as being the senior Colonel to take command of this party, as likewise to Colonel Vermuyden for that party of 2,500 horse and dragoons, and in case the King should draw out the garrison of Newark we have written to Colonel Rossiter for 600 horse of Lincolnshire. You are therefore to come with all diligence to such a general rendezvous as Sir John Gell shall appoint. . '

The King's appearance at Ashby on the 27th created understandable consternation. The Newark horse slipped out and joined his veteran army whilst the Parliamentarian garrison at Coleorton fled in panic. Gell apprehensively awaited the promised reinforcements from the surrounding counties and sat tight at Derby, fearing that Charles would march north and acting on Hastings's advice, storm the town.

The Parliamentary scouts reported that some 2,000 of the King's horse faced Derby and Gell's worst fears seemed about to materialise. The Barton garrison watching Tutbury Castle was called in and Gell ordered the constables of the neighbouring areas to send all well-affected men to Derby with their arms 'to do service for the State.'

Royalist patrols severed all communication with the outside

world; Gell's letters remained unanswered and he could give no news of Derby's fate to the House.

In fact, it was the threatening of Oxford by the New Model Army that persuaded Charles to retire; with his capital in danger, the King left off his deliberations regarding Derby and so the town was spared the attentions of an enemy yet again. The contrast with the fate of neighbouring county towns is instructive.

The king's military secretary Sir Edward Walker commented: 'It is verily thought if . . . Derby had been summoned, Sir John Gell would have rendered it; but Prince Rupert would not do it, out of this punctilio of honour, that if he had sent a summons he was obliged (if he was repulsed) to besiege it . . .'

Clearly, the Royalists could ill afford such an expense of time whilst Oxford was imperilled.

Curious evidence of Rupert's interest in Derby consists of an astrological prediction cast by Elias Ashmole and dated 27th April 1645, titled:

'About ye town of Derby . . If prince Robert would storm the town and if yes. Quid agendum.' Particularly puzzling is the date of the prediction, for on 27th April the Prince is believed to have been in the Worcester/Hereford region. He was certainly at Worcester on the 20th and arrived in Oxford on the 4th May, a week after the chart was drawn. Is it feasible to think of Rupert meditating an attack on Derby — a middling sort of Parliamentary garrison town — when the King himself had no clear strategic aim when marching out from Oxford on the 7th? If Ashmole's April is a clerical error for May, then the quid agendum has far more significance, for on 27th May the Royalist army was marching from Ashby to Loughborough. Lord Loughborough (Henry Hastings) was in attendance on the King with units of his North Midlands Army containing numerous Derbyshire officers besides those who had ridden in from Newark garrison under Sir Marmaduke Langdale. Now surely was the time for Hastings and his Derbyshire men to press Rupert for a decision on Derby, which unlike its neighbours, had uniquely avoided Royalist attack since the beginning of the war. Unfortunately there is no way of knowing whether or not Ashmole made a mistake in writing

April instead of May, though the exigencies of the military situation would seem to suggest so. In any event, on the 28th, Rupert led his cavalry down to Leicester and on the 30th the town was taken by storm by the Royalist army. Any lingering hopes entertained by the Derbyshire Royalists that Gell would finally be ousted, were dashed by Naseby's verdict.

As the King withdrew from the borders of Derbyshire, Gell was commanded to effect a rendezvous at Nottingham with all the forces previously assigned to him by the CBK and to pursue the King as he marched towards Leicester. For reasons as yet inexplicable, Gell tarried at Nottingham and was slow to obey his instructions. Though he had a good body of some 2,000 horse and dragoons, he delayed shadowing the Royalists, preferring to await the arrival of the full reinforcement commanded from the neighbouring County Committees. Thus he failed to reach Naseby on the 4th June. However, though absenting himself from the battlefield, he was in an excellent position to cut off the Royalist retreat and to seize the most valued prize of all — Charles himself. But the King evaded Gell and capture with suspicious ease.

Two days after the battle, Parliamentarian news-sheets reported that Gell had taken some 200 of the King's horse and had also defeated a party of Newarkers escaping from the debacle and running for home. Yet Joshua Sprigge in 'Anglia Rediviva' remarks that: 'It was the wonder of all men how they (being in such a tired and distracted condition) could escape Sir John Gell's horse, who the same day were on their march from Nottingham towards Leicester.'

Though Fairfax and the CBK expressed themselves pleased that Sir John had 'arrived so opportunely,' Cromwell himself is said to have 'soundly chid' Gell for not more vigorously intercepting the King's forces on their way back to Leicester and that thereafter, Gell was 'suspected to be a well wisher to the King's party.'

What was the truth of all this? Could Gell have earned undying fame as the man who ended the civil war by taking the King prisoner? Gell himself years later partially explains his conduct when making two specific references to this incident during his trial for misprision of treason in 1650 and wrote in his response to the Breda Declaration:

'Upon my examination Sir Henry Mildmay did charge me that at the Battle of Naseby his late Majesty was routed and that I had a brigade of two thousand horse and was near the King's party and would not interrupt his late Majesty; which was true enough.' Referring to Cromwell's criticism he continues: 'The late Protector and I was ever adversaries and he at the siege and regaining of Leicester, caused my regiment of horse to be taken from me. I then refused to pursue his late Majesty to Worcester.'

After Naseby, Gell's horse stood on the north side of Leicester, which Lord Loughborough wisely surrendered to Fairfax's army on 18th June. The garrison of some 1600 men marched out only with staves in their hands. They left 30 colours, all their weapons and 500 valuable horses. Loughborough and the die-hards pressed on to Ashby, resolved to defend the Castle and continue the war. Gell reports his fall from grace with, 'Fairfax dismissed Colonel Gell and all the fforces that were under his command.' (TR).

Despite which, upon his return to Derby, the CBK immediately ordered him to march with his horse and dragoons to Coventry where he was to re-unite with the forces that had formerly been under his command, as per the instructions of the CBK before Naseby.

Gell dutifully set out and tells us that when he reached Sinfin Moor just two miles south of Derby, 'part of his horse began to mutinie for want of money.' (TR).

He pressed on however with 2 or 3 troops via Lichfield and so reached Coventry, where he 'tarried there ten dayes and noebody coming to him hee returned backe again to Derby.'

Major Sanders sheds some explanatory light upon these events and wrote to his friend Captain Nathaniel Barton that when he arrived in Derby from Gloucester — where he had been seeking employment in the New Model Army and where Barton apparently remained — some of the horse troopers, upon hearing of his arrival, set up the cry of 'A Sanders!' and said that they would march no further without their Major. They turned about, despite all that Sir John could do, and marched back to Derby. Sanders tells us that Sir John was obliged to continue his journey to Coventry with only his own troop and that of his loyal follower, Captain Rhodes. The rest of the regiment abandoned Gell completely, their Colonel smarting no doubt over this flouting of his authority by the Sanders supporters within his regiment. Small wonder that Gell glosses over this insubordination in TR as being simply a dispute over pay.

Sanders told Barton that he had the remaining nine troops of the regiment at his command, all wearing the colours of Fairfax in their hats, whereas Gell's men wore their Colonel's and called Sanders's men 'rogues,' and threatened to pull them out. Sanders entreated Barton to intercede with Fairfax and Cromwell to 'get more command of the (Derby) horse' and to use his good endeavours to get the regiment made over to Sanders and added to the New Model horse.

JULY 1645 — THE KING'S PEREGRINATIONS

On the 16th July, Sir John Frescheville's Major of Horse, the Walloon John Jammot, suddenly recaptured Welbeck House. Frescheville then installed himself with a garrison of 250 foot and levied contributions throughout north Derbyshire for the upkeep of this new satellite garrison of Newark.

For the past year, Frescheville had oscillated in his loyalty after the shock of Marston Moor and had surrendered his house at Staveley when called upon to do so by Fairfax. However, finding it impossible to come to a satisfactory accommodation with Parliament, he threw in his lot once more with the King.

It was the Royalist seizure of Welbeck that curbed the incipient fracturing of Gell's regiment of horse. The warring factions united against the common enemy and under Gell's personal command, made a rendezvous at Wingfield Manor with the Nottingham forces under Colonel Thornhagh. The allies failed to retake the place by a surprise attack and so contented themselves with encountering the enemy once or twice and taking 'many prisoners.' (TR).

The King's arrival at Tutbury from Lichfield on the 12th August caused the Nottingham and Derby forces to separate and the latter fell back to Derby. Gell's scouts reported that the King's army, numbering about 2,000 — 'for the most part ill armed and ill horsed' — was marching through Derbyshire to Chatsworth. Sir John once again (and doubtless much to the chagrin of Thomas Sanders and others of the win-the war outright party) did but little to discomfort Charles on his passage, but a forlorn hope of troopers tackled the Royalist rearguard with more valour than discretion. Symonds relates that on the march from Tutbury to Ashbourne, a 'body of 500 of the enemy's horse fell upon our rear, near Barton garrison, by Tedbury; were well received by us, twenty of ours hurt, three or four on both sides killed; we took twelve prisoners and lost some.'

Gell says only 100 of his cavalry took part in this attack, which may have been the work of Captain Barton, the appropriately named governor of the garrison, or even Sanders — hence Gell's disapproval. Once more, Gell excused his inactivity by blaming the tardiness of his neighbours in Yorkshire, Nottinghamshire and Leicester, who failed to act on his early intelligence and concentrate their forces. Had they done so, Gell claimed, he could have 'rendered His Majesty unto his Parliament.'

In fact, Charles's small but rapacious army stripped Derbyshire of vital provisions and transported them to Newark, stopping on the 15th at Welbeck. This was more than guerilla plundering and should perhaps be seen as the resurrection of the Royalist financial administrative system of 1643-4, though now centred upon Newark. Gell now found himself paralysed by a second mutiny in the Horse regiment and could therefore do nothing — assuming he wished to — about the revival of Royalist activity in Derbyshire

Charles made good his escape from Newark on the 22nd and so continued his journeying in spite of Gell being given command of the forces of Derbyshire, Staffordshire, Lincolnshire and Nottinghamshire for the purposes of stopping him. Having failed utterly in this vital task, Gell was replaced by Sydenham Poyntz and ordered to provide 400 horse for his army. He once again procrastinated and received a stern reprimand from the CBK, ordering him to despatch the 400 horse at once. Sir John finally complied and this contingent served under Poyntz at the siege of Chester and went on to participate in the defeat of the King's forces at Rowton Moor on 24th September in which they 'utterlie Rowted, wounded, kild and scattered all the Kinges forces.'

Gell says nothing of this in his True Relation; instead he deliberates on the local conflict with Tutbury Castle. The Staffordshire Committee agreed a joint enterprise with Gell and the latter sent 400 men under his brother to plan a siege. The estimate arrived at by the council of war was that at least a month would be required. Neither party could afford such a delay and neither were they strong enough to risk a storm, so, mindful of an earlier command from Poyntz that 700 foot should be ready at an hour's notice to march against Newark, Gell's troops marched home having achieved nothing.

Two days later the King once more appeared and passed within eight miles of Derby en route for Newark. His arrival there emboldened the Newarkers to despatch Colonel John Shallcross with 300 men to seize and garrison Chatsworth. Their commander had first served as Lieutenant Colonel to John Milward when he formed his regiment in late 1643 and had been based then at Chatsworth with Eyre's regiment. Both had gone north to Marston Moor, after which Milward submitted to Parliament and Shallcross — now High Sheriff of Derbyshire — took command of the regiment. He served with the Northern Horse under Langdale at Naseby and was a seasoned campaigner. It may well have been at this time that he returned to his home, Shallcross Hall near Whaley Bridge, then garrisoned by some of Colonel Randle Ashenhurst's men and surprised the defenders. One of these soldiers, James Cawyerd, in a petition for relief to the Derbyshire Sessions in 1649 recounts:

'Mr. Shallcross himself entringe the house and a strong party with him cutt and wounded most of the souldiers found in the house: Amongst whom yor peticioner received such cutts and woundes that ever since hee hath lost the use of his Arme & hand to his utter undoinge: without some speedie relief he beinge by p'fession a blacksmith . . '

After the raid, Shallcross returned to Chatsworth to counter an attack by Major Molanus and 400 Derby foot. The skirmishing went on for a fortnight before the Roundheads repossessed the House and beat off Shallcross's horsemen.

OCTOBER, NOVEMBER, DECEMBER 1645
NEWARK AGAIN

Until Newark could be taken, satellite and subordinate garrisons like Welbeck and Chatsworth would continue to spring up and devour the countryside of the tribute urgently required by the Parliament's forces. Poyntz therefore began in earnest his campaign against the Cavalier's 'Key to the North.' He began on 15th October to assemble his army at Derby and was provided with 500 of Gell's foot as ordered by Parliament. Meanwhile, six of the nine troops of horse were sent back to serve with Brereton's army and the remaining three, together with the rest of the foot, went under the command of Lieutenant Colonel Thomas Gell to blockade Welbeck; other units of horse continued to occupy Barton House in order to constrain the Tutbury garrison and prevent them from levying contributions on the surrounding territory. Derby was thus denuded of troops and Gell was compelled to call in remnants of the trained bands to secure the town against a possible Royalist coup.

The Derby forces of horse and foot were scattered far and wide, serving in Leicestershire (Coleorton and the Vale of Belvoir), Nottinghamshire (Newark and Shelford) and Cheshire and North Wales. Only the small garrisons of Barton, Wingfield and Derby remained within the county, along with Sir John himself. The Derbyshire forces gave good service in all three theatres as the civil war was fought to its bloody and now predictable finish.

The six troops of horse under Major Sanders in Cheshire — (some 150 men) — were sent by Brereton into North Wales where, together with neighbouring county auxiliary horse regiments, they inflicted a decisive defeat on Sir William Vaughan at the Battle of Denbigh. Brereton himself reported that Sanders, with the Derby and Warwickshire horse, pursued the enemy to the walls of Conway Castle, taking no less than three or four hundred of the enemy horse as his prisoners and was a 'faithful and gallant officer.' Sanders appears to have remained with six troops under Brereton until Chester finally surrendered on 3rd February 1646.

From 28th October 1645, the foot, commanded by Major Molanus, served on the 'Newark Front' under Poyntz and on 3rd of November, took part in the particularly savage attack on Shelford Manor, another Newark satellite. The governor, Colonel Philip Stanhope and his garrison of some 200 men, including part of the Queen's Regiment, were refused quarter and all but 40 were put to the sword. That night Charles left Newark as Shelford burned and reached Oxford two days later. A second garrison at Wiverton fell on the 9th and on the 22nd, the Derby foot stormed the outworks of Belvoir Castle, losing some 11 men killed and 27 wounded in the desperate attempt. Gell records:

'. . for their service and valor in storming the said workes, the Parliament bestowed £40 amongst (the) Derby souldyers to drinke.' (TR).

Meanwhile Lieutenant Colonel Gell's detachment watching Welbeck persuaded Frescheville to surrender on 13th November. Perhaps the dreadful news of Shelford's fate had a sufficiently salutory effect. The garrison rendered up the house after its arrears of contribution taxes had been paid by the victors and then marched into Newark, after which a chastened Frescheville fled the place and escaped for Holland. His retirement from Welbeck left Tutbury and Newark as the only local havens for Derbyshire Royalists still in arms. But many of their number now began to contact the Derby Committee, putting out feelers with a view to compounding and retiring from a war they now saw as irretrievably lost.

The noose was tightening around the 'Key to the North.' Gell's brother, Thomas now brought his troops from Welbeck to join Molanus and the rest of the regiment before Newark and Poyntz's army was met there by the Scottish army on 26th November. Refusing to be overawed by the numbers gathering against them, the Newarkers launched 400 horse and 1000 foot in a surprise night attack on the 1st January, 1646, their target being Poyntz's headquarters at the village of East Stoke. The Nottinghamshire and Derbyshire soldiers, numbering 500 or so, were left to fend for themselves when their accompanying horse fled the field, but Gell recounts that 'In this skirmish (the) Derbyshire foot stood most valiantly and courageously too it, soe that as soone as it was day, Colonell General Poyntz gave them many thanks in the open field where they stood in battalio, for their courage and valor.' (TR). However, Royalist sources state that only 300 foot and 800 horse sallied out and took between 100 and 220 prisoners, after surprising Poyntz in his house and making him run away without his boots, leaving his house to be ransacked and his money taken by the Cavaliers.

Gell's narrative of events contained in his 'True Relation' abruptly terminates at this point. Perhaps this was due to the accusations now pouring in against him by the Derby Committee and finding their way to London. His actions from this point onwards became highly tendentious and were to land him in trouble, not only with the locals who were clamouring for the revocation of his governorship — but also with Brereton and the Committee of Both Kingdoms.

Gell self-evidently wrote his 'True Relation' as a vindication of his career and as a defence to the charges that were soon to be laid against him. No wonder indeed that he concludes his version of events with a highly-coloured account of the fight at East Stoke and omits all mention of his own activities thereafter during 1646.

PART VII

TUTBURY and GELL'S DISMISSAL

JANUARY 1646 — TUTBURY

Ever since a detachment of Manchester's army had broken the Derbyshire Royalist garrisons after Marston Moor, Gell had hungered to settle with the occupiers of Tutbury Castle. Time and time again he had been distracted from this objective by what he perceived as the outside interference of Brereton, Fairfax and the CBK, to say nothing of the irritation and opposition posed by Major Sanders and his captains of horse. Their Independent tendencies, in both politics and religion, had threatened on several occasions to undermine his authority. Now, finally, with Sanders in the leaguer before Chester, and with no further demands being made on him by the CBK, he sought to return to his long cherished objective.

Tutbury Castle had been much weakened both by plague and by Loughborough's drawing out of fit men in a vain attempt to break the siege of Chester. The Staffordshire local forces had made an attempt on the Castle at the beginning of the year but had been repulsed. Gell now appeared on the 14th with the few forces he was still free to dispose of and 'surprised the town and took 140 horse and diverse prisoners, killed some and wounded many.' He returned again five days later and beat up the town but failed to take the Castle, which was still too strong for his weak command. Parliament at this early stage in the Tutbury proceedings approved his initiative and sent him a supply of powder and match as encouragement.

Captain Rhodes's troop was established at Barton House to harass the garrison's foraging parties. This it did on 16th February when the garrison of Tutbury sought to bring in some stores from Uttoxeter assisted by a party of Newark horse. Neither side could claim a victory, the only losers being the unfortunate inhabitants of Boylestone and Marchington, who found themselves obliged to pay contributions to both Tutbury and Barton.

Gell then made preparations for an attack on Ashby but with the fall of Chester on 3rd February, Loughborough's men returned from their abortive relief operation and beefed up the garrison. From Chester too came Gell's six troops of Derbyshire horse but before Gell could employ them against Tutbury, Brereton recalled them to assist in the reduction of Lichfield Close, which began in earnest on 9th March.

Tutbury Castle from a 1733 engraving, purporting to show the defences in their pre Civil War glory

On the 24th, Gell's troops carried out a successful assault on the town of Tutbury when the Derby foot and some 200 Staffordshire horse swept into the town centre and after a desperate encounter, overthrew a fort that the defenders had erected at the market cross. The fort was dismantled and the attackers withdrew to Barton with 30 prisoners. The Parliamentarian 'Weekly Account' for February 26-March 4th attributes this victory to Captain William Rhodes of Steetley, Gell's only friend amongst the Derby captains of horse. However, in a later communication to the House by Major Sanders, the honour is attributed to Captain Greenwood of

Ashbourne and no mention whatever is made of Rhodes. Sanders's account alleges that Gell was up to his old trick of bribing the London pamphleteers. He describes the action at Tutbury as follows:

'Captain Greenwood, who is governor of Barton Garrison, an honest, valiant man who hath commission under Major Sanders, he with his troop consisting of a 100 horse, old and valiant soldiers, being all dismounted, first entered the town being seconded with Captain Villiers and 20 horse . . . We marched up the great street to the cross and possessed ourselves of the guard, a serjeant . . . We took about 2 prisoners and about 120 horse. This is the truth of the business, whatever others may say or arrogate to themselves. This was thought good to be manifested to the world to show the arrogance of some who have all the praise and merit least.

So we poor lambs bear on our backs
Wool to clothe other idle Jacks.

. . . This is the first vizard that we pulled off from Sir John Gell's face, who the pamphleteers cry up for 'Active,' who never but once at Saltheath (ie the battle of Hopton Heath) looked one enemy in the face. This is the truth from the hands of those that will justify it.'

GELL'S INCREASING UNPOPULARITY

Unrest and resentment had been seething in Derby since November 1645 when the Recruiter election set the Gell faction and its opponents against each other's throats. From the first, Gell had dominated the Derby Committee, packing it with his nominees like Sir John Curzon MP, Sir George Gresley, his brother Thomas the lawyer and his two sons in law, Henry Wigfall and John Wigley. The town's other MP was Nathaniel Hallowes — the only Derby man on the Committee — who, like Curzon, fed the House and London press with generous propaganda praising Gell's military exploits. As time wore on, complaints increased that Gell convened the Committee irregularly, gave it no fixed meeting place and kept no records of its business. It was certainly used by Gell to divert the rents and proceeds of sequestered

Derbyshire Royalists into his own pocket and those of his supporters. Even the money and pay infrequently sent up from London to pay the soldiers was bestowed largely on those companies and troops of horse who obeyed him without question. Gradually opposition to Gell's autocratic rule began to coalesce around Thomas Sanders and those of his party who wanted more open local government, religious independency and a more outright and decisive prosecution of the war. This faction included most of the captains of horse, Robert Mellor — a captain of foot — together with another wealthy burgess, Gervase Bennett.

Following Gell's arrest of Sanders previously referred to, the Earl of Essex and the House insisted that he, together with Mellor and Bennett, be included amongst the Committee men. This so incensed Gell that he was heard to say that he would rather fight with Major Sanders than with 'any Cavalier in England and that he would have his pennyworth out of him.'

He is also reported as turning on Bennett the new Treasurer and declaring that he would turn Derby into a Royalist fort! When asked by the Treasurer what would then become of Derby, Gell snapped: 'I care not. Let it hang itself as it will.'

This quarrel between the rival factions came to a head in November, 1645, when an election was fixed for Derby to send a 'recuiter' to Westminster to fill the vacancy left by the Royalist MP, William Allestry, who had joined the King's 'mongrel Parliament' at Oxford.

The poll was to take place on 12th November. The Gell faction put up Lieutenant Colonel Thomas Gell and the contender, supported by the Sanders clique, was Captain Robert Mellor. Both sides resorted to all manner of threats and irregularities but the most dramatic was engineered by the town's governor, Sir John himself. The election coincided with a demand from Colonel General Poyntz to send more troops from Derby to the 'Newark Front,' so Gell cynically despatched Captain Mellor and his company, thus at a stroke removing his enemy and a goodly number of burgesses who had expressed their determination to vote for their Captain. Thomas Gell's company however, remained in the town, but unlike Mellor's, consisted largely of soldiers raised from Gell's estates around Wirksworth who were thus ineligible to vote. Another body of foot, commanded by one Robert Freland — a Captain in Thomas Gell's company — marched into the market square with drums beating and matches lit, to intimidate the voters who wished to elect Mellor. Tempers ran high and one of the townsmen is recorded as declaring to another, who intended to vote for Gell:

'Why will you do so wicked a thing? He that stands for Gell stands for the Devil, for he is a worthless man and a man of no trust. They that give their voice for him to do damn themselves and their posterity to the Pit of Hell!'

Sir John tried to overawe the voters by pointedly making notes of all those who voted against his brother. In the end, however, the tellers reported 170 votes for Thomas Gell and 149 for Mellor. In spite of this, Bennett, the mayor and a strong supporter of Mellor, declared Mellor the victor. The whole sordid matter had to be examined by Parliament's Committee of Privileges which finally pronounced that Thomas Gell was the duly elected candidate.

Such were the divisions within the ranks of Derby's Parliamentarians.

MARCH, APRIL 1646 — TUTBURY AGAIN

Whoever it was who led the successful attack on Tutbury, Rhodes or Greenwood, the result was a severe setback for governor Kniveton, whose soldiers now began to desert and whose foraging parties were speedily intercepted by the troopers stationed for that purpose at Barton House. Plague took hold in the Castle and food began to run out; Gell estimated in March that the place was manned by only 60 horse and 120 foot.

Gell was eager to be in at what he fondly believed would be the final kill but once again, he was to be disappointed, for on 13th March Brereton's second in command, Colonel Bowyer, arrived from the siege of Lichfield with orders to take charge of operations around Tutbury. A week later, Kniveton's Lieutenant Moore and 22 of the garrison gave themselves up to Bowyer's men, but a surrender of Kniveton's entire force was postponed by the inevitable squabbling between Gell and

Brereton as to who should treat with the defenders. The latter were fully aware of the gravity of their situation. On 28th February their overall area commander, Lord Loughborough, had finally given up and surrendered Ashby Castle; it now remained only to emulate him and seek to obtain the best possible terms. Here it seemed that the conflict between Gell and Brereton might well work to the advantage of the beleagured Royalists.

Brereton rightly argued that administratively the Castle lay within Staffordshire and thus fell within his jurisdiction as commander of that county's forces. Gell however, felt that as most of the garrison's officers and men were Derbyshire Royalists, they should negotiate with him and not Brereton's Colonel Bowyer. Furthermore, he claimed that his former frequent attacks and raids on the place and his establishment of Barton house as a garrison of observation, had established his right to oversee the termination of the enterprise. Much blood, time and treasure had been expended by the Derbyshire forces against the Castle and Gell determined that he alone should reap the reward of its capture.

Whilst Brereton was tied down with the siege of Lichfield Close, Gell undertook to act behind his back and try to reach an accommodation with the defenders. So, on 6th April, he offered the governor 14 Articles of surrender which in effect, amounted to nothing less than a free pardon for the Royalists, provided they capitulated at once. He even went so far as to promise to 'take off fines and sequestrations' levied on the estates of the officers and to grant them 6 months rent due from their tenants. They were assured 'that not any commander, gentleman and soldier shall be hereafter troubled or questioned for any hostile act done by any of them during the war.'

When Brereton heard of these terms, he promptly quit the siegeworks at Lichfield and hastened over to Tutbury to confront Gell. Parliament meanwhile castigated Gell for the unwarranted leniency of his terms which had been communicated to the House and sent him a strongly worded letter of rebuke:

'We have seen the articles treated by you with the governor of Tutbury, the matter whereof we wholly dislike; neither did we ever give you any power to treat about it. We had formerly committed that service to Sir William Brereton and others and have again recommended it to him . . . . to transact according to our former instructions. We therefore desire you to give no interruption or impediment to that work but to leave it to them to proceed in. We desire that the Derbyshire horse which are at that service may continue there for the finishing of the service.'

Far from being intimidated by this reprimand and by Brereton's reassertion of command, Gell continued to defy Brereton in his absence at Lichfield, even though the latter declared Gell's Articles to be 'the strangest and most dishonourable articles that I have ever seen.'

Major Shaw, one of Brereton's officers, complained that Gell insisted on commanding the Derby horse in person and would brook no interference by Brereton's nominees; further, he had taken Sir Andrew Kniveton to Barton House for negotiations, 'where I hear they are very pleasant together.'

Shaw wrote to Brereton again to describe how Gell had apparently slipped into the Castle with Sir John Harpur, past the Staffordshire guards, and held a conference with the garrison's senior officers. Upon their return, 'our guard beat them off, not knowing who they were.' After this, Gell was much discontented because 'he was opposed and hindered from going to the Castle' and threatened Shaw that he would abandon the siege altogether if crossed again.

What is one to make of this almost farcical situation? It seems that Gell, in effect, had had enough of the war. He did not want a showdown with the King to the bitter end and only wanted some sort of acceptable Presbyterian church settlement, plus financial recompense for all his efforts to date. Like most of his class, he feared the New Model Army and its sectarian apologists and by 1646 felt he had done more than his fair share for an ungrateful Parliament. Thus negotiations with Kniveton were an attempt to bring the war locally to an end and to win for himself fame as the conqueror of Tutbury. Perhaps — knowing his avaricious character — there was also an attempt to bribe the garrison into yielding hard cash in exchange for easy terms. For their part, the defenders sought to play off Gell against Brereton in order to win the most favourable terms possible.

When it became apparent that Gell's proposals would not be ratified by Parliament, the governor of Tutbury requested negotiations with Brereton's Colonel Bowyer, who returned from Lichfield to treat on the 16th April. Even so, Gell was still anxious to reach an accommodation with the defenders and Brereton's Letter Book refers to constant 'private plots and contrivements' between the Derby troops and the garrison, whereby officers were let into the Castle with letters from Sir John Gell and messengers were let down the wall with ropes. Bowyer complained in despair that the work of securing a surrender could only go forward if the Derbyshire forces were to be removed altogether and sent away home!

Finally, Brereton came in person on the 20th to sanction Bowyer's new articles. He learned in detail of Gell's interference and when sending a copy of Bowyer's articles of surrender to London to obtain Parliament's approval, he added his own report on Gell's behaviour, accusing him of jeopardizing the whole operation through his refusal to obey the Committee's orders.

The revised articles were approved by the CBK and on the 21st April, the remains of the garrison marched out and Gell was put to work slighting the Castle's defences as bidden by Parliament. Originally, Sir John had sought to preserve the structure, being well aware of its status as a Royal stronghold, but the Committee wrote ordering the destruction of the Castle and delivered a second warning to Gell. Brereton's criticisms had borne fruit and the CBK demanded an explanation from Gell for his wayward behaviour. By now, accusations against him were legion and the Committee of Examinations was busy collecting evidence. We may safely speculate that Gell was indifferent to all this — his actual response to this further reprimand is not recorded — but he had been put in his place by Brereton and the CBK and was still woefully in arrears with his pay. It must have been here at Tutbury, as he smarted under what he felt to be Parliament's harsh ill-usage of him, that Sir John slowly began to discover himself a Royalist sympathiser. After all, the war was won and like Essex, Gell believed that enough had been gained to make an acceptable peace with the King.

At this point, in early May, Gell was summoned to appear before the Committee of Privileges in London, to answer a battery of charges in the long-maturing case against him. In September he was stripped of his governorship and as a consequence, his political and military powerbase in Derby was finally overthrown.

PART VIII

FINALE

MAY, OCTOBER 1646 — DISBANDMENT

The forces that Gell had raised in the service of Parliament were no longer needed once Newark gave in to Poyntz on 8th May and Lichfield surrendered to Brereton on 10th July, and so Gell's regiments of horse and foot converged on Derby, their fighting done, to demand payment. Both regiments were grossly in arrears and roamed the town in open mutiny. In the past, by threats, cajolery and sheer force of personality, their Colonel had managed to suppress indiscipline. Now he was in London answering the various charges of his enemies and there was no-one able to command their obedience. At Wingfield Manor, the governor and former commander of Gell's artillery, Captain German Pole, was locked in his chamber and held there by the rebellious garrison until the soldiers were assured that their arrears would be paid.

Some £5,000 was eventually granted by Parliament on 23rd June to pay off the Derby horse and foot, most of this being met from fines levied on the property of Sir John Harpur of Swarkestone and Sir Henry Hunloke of Wingerworth, the balance to be met from sequestered Church lands. The three Derby MPs, Sir John Curzon, Sir John Coke, and Nathaniel Hallowes were ordered to see the business done as swiftly as possible and they resolved to pay the soldiers off whilst in their respective quarters rather than to risk bringing them, as customary, to a general pay muster in the town.

Whilst Gell's veterans were being hurriedly disbanded, the Committee for Affairs in Ireland sought volunteers from the

Derby forces and managed to raise a body of foot under the newly promoted Colonel Robert Freland, while a small party of horse was re-engaged and also sent to Ireland under Colonel Samuel Roper of Heanor.

In London, on 8th October, Gell received a letter from the clerk of his own troop of horse, telling him of its dispersal and of the horse regiment's disbandment. He was also sent a list dated 29th October referring to his foot company, recording the details of those who had been discharged, those who since August had been re-mustered for service in Ireland, those who had deserted and those who had died.

During the previous month, Gell was stripped of his governorship. In reaching this decision, the Committee was no doubt impressed by the scathing indictment placed before it by Major Sanders, which amongst other things accused Gell of unlawful imprisonment, misappropriation of public money, disobedience to CBK instructions, non-payment of commanders of horse, military mismanagement and a scandalous life-style — including swearing, profanity, 'cavalierish' behaviour, persecution of Godly men and the favouring

Mugginton church, burial place of Col. Thomas Sanders. He built a family vault here in 1651 to the north of the chancel. He did better than Gell out of the war, amassed a rich estate and outlived his old antagonist by 24 years. His buffcoat now resides in the National Army Museum.

of delinquents and malignants. Gell counterclaimed for expenses amounting to £7,000 in arrears of pay and a further £5,000 for his plundered estate and loss of revenue therefrom. However, the Committee of Account declared that between 1st November, 1642, and 6th September, 1646, Gell had spent only £3,000 in the public service, which was ordered to be repaid with interest at 8%.

Enraged, Gell employed the next three years struggling to recover his lost revenues and endeavouring to vindicate his wartime career. It was probably about this time in autumn 1646 that he composed his 'True Relation.'

From September onwards he lived in London, but his strenuous campaign to re-establish himself, recover his alleged losses and to win recognition, did not succeed. He had made too many powerful enemies. His regiments of horse and foot were now disbanded and scattered, his political power finished in Derby where now his opponents held sway. He could expect nothing from Brereton or Fairfax, with both of whom he'd crossed swords at one time or another, and the neighbouring Committee at Nottingham damned him as a meddler, whilst Cromwell himself had castigated Gell for his indolence after Naseby.

Whilst in London, Gell ran across Sanders and his friend Barton who were attending the King's trial. In a letter to his son dated 16th January 1649, Gell wrote:

'The Chancery and the King's bench is making ready for trial of the King and others also; but the King is such a high thing that the others is not spoken of . . . . Sanders and Barton do sometimes spend their opinions and censure the King deeply. So you have their verdict already.'

Whilst the King was imprisoned on the isle of Wight, Gell contrived to send him money and took special care to get and preserve receipts for at least £300 — bearing the King's signature — which would stand him in good stead with the Royalist underground and act as an insurance policy for the future. The impecunious Charles chose to forget that he had excluded Gell from his General Pardon to Derbyshire in 1643 due to the latter's treatment of the Earl of Northampton's body after the battle of Hopton Heath.

After the King's execution and a Commons order dated

23rd February finally stripping him of all his commissions, Gell began actively to associate with the Royalist enemies of the Commonwealth. He was imprisoned in the Tower for seven months in September 1650, charged with Treason and misprision (concealment) of Treason.

The case against him for participation in the plot to seize Kings Lynn and let in Charles II, collapsed on a technicality but he was committed to the Tower for life on 27th September, convicted of misprision. Constant petitions pleading his poor state of health led to release in 1652, after serving only two years of his sentence and on 18th April he was pardoned under the Great Seal. Thereafter he sought solace for his declining health by frequent and expensive forays to Bath, where he spent considerable sums on treatment for palsy.

At the Restoration, his receipts to Charles I and his imprisonment in the Tower served him well and when Charles II landed at Dover, he sprang out of retirement, petitioned for a pardon on 4th June 1660 (which was granted on 17th November) and for his 'loyalty' was sworn a Gentleman of the Privy Chamber Extraordinary. One can only wonder at the reactions of genuine and devoted Derbyshire Royalists to this seemingly miraculous elevation of their former enemy.

Sir Andrew Kniveton for example, was compelled to sell his estates and died a forgotten pauper in 1672; so too did Aston Cockayne of Ashbourne, who had also served in the Tutbury garrison and died penniless in a Derby lodging house in 1684.

Sir John Gell died on 26th October 1671, aged 78, at his house in St. Martin's Lane and his body was brought back to St. Mary's church at Wirksworth for interment, where, as Trevor Brighton fittingly remarks:

'There may have been many dutiful mourners and doubtless there were the usual panegyrics; there can have been few genuine tears.'

Not surprisingly, Gell's elaborate sepulchral monument was soon allegedly defaced by his enemies; a simple tablet on the east wall of the choir now marks the grave of this unlamented but remarkable man.

The final resting place of Sir John Gell, St. Mary's, Wirksworth. His small memorial tablet is quite dwarfed by those of his lesser-known ancestors

CHRONOLOGY

22 August 1642	—	King Charles raises his Royal Standard at Nottingham
15 September	—	Charles enters Derby
20 "	—	Charles reaches Shrewsbury
23 "	—	Rupert's success at Powick Bridge, Worcester
27 "	—	Gell obtains colonel's commission from Essex
11 October	—	Gell collects greycoat foot company from Hull
12 "	—	Charles marches from Shrewsbury towards London
23 "	—	Battle of Edgehill; inconclusive
25 "	—	Essex retires to Warwick
26 "	—	Gell arrives at Wirksworth
29 "	—	King Charles occupies Oxford
31 "	—	Gell enters Derby
3 November	—	Charles marches from Oxford to London
10 "	—	Colonel Gell gives out commission to his captains
12 "	—	Prince Rupert storms Brentford
13 "	—	Essex and the London Trained Bands face the King at Turnham Green; London defies the King
25 "	—	Gell's regiment is fully recruited
29 "	—	The King falls back from Reading to Oxford
December	—	The Derby regiment attacks the Earl of Chesterfield's house at Bretby
"	—	Newcastle's Sir John Henderson appointed governor of Royalist Newark
"	—	The Derby forces aid Nottingham allies in raising a regiment of foot and building defensive works
3 "	—	The Earl of Newcastle's army enters York
7 "	—	Newcastle's Royal army marches south and takes Tadcaster from Fairfax
15 "	—	Derbyshire incorporated in the Parliamentarian East Midlands Association

---

3-7 January 1643	—	Gell clashes with Hastings at Swarkestone
17 "	—	EMA contingents attack Hastings at Ashby
23 "	—	Sir Thomas Fairfax takes Leeds and Wakefield and Newcastle retreats to York
"	—	Belvoir, Wiverton and Shelford garrisoned for the King as satellites of Newark
15 February	—	Gell plunders Stanhope's manor at Elvaston
22 "	—	The Queen lands at Bridlington with war supplies and munitions for the King
25 "	—	Hastings promoted Colonel General
28 "	—	Derby forces join Ballard's abortive attack on Newark and are repulsed
2-5 March	—	First siege of Lichfield Close; Earl of Chesterfield (Stanhope) surrenders to Gell
19 "	—	Battle of Hopton Heath (Saltheath) A draw
21 April	—	Prince Rupert retakes Lichfield
May	—	Captain Sanders, stationed by Gell at Burton, defects to Staffordshire Committee
"	—	EMA forces "promenade" in the Vale of Belvoir
13 . "	—	Action at Grantham; Cromwell's first success
21 "	—	Fairfax captures Wakefield
16 June/3 July	—	Queen and her army at Newark
21 June	—	Newark Royalists attack Nottingham
30 "	—	Battle of Adwalton Moor; Fairfax defeated
7 July	—	Queen storms Burton on Trent; Sanders taken
8 "	—	Derby forces attack Wooton Lodge, Staffs.
26 "	—	Rupert captures Bristol
6 August	—	Newcastle takes Lincoln
10 August/5 September	—	Siege of Gloucester
18 September	—	Newark Royalists enter and loot Nottingham; Derby forces provide assistance
20 "	—	First Battle of Newbury; King v Essex; a draw
October	—	Sir Richard Byron made governor of Newark
11 "	—	Colonel Cromwell wins cavalry action at Winceby
16 "	—	Sanders promoted Major and added to Derby Committee and begins to raise horse regiment
23 "	—	Henry Hastings created Baron Loughborough
27 "	—	Charles makes Newcastle a marquis
December	—	Newcastle's troops invade Derbyshire
15 "	—	Sir Francis Mackworth takes Wingfield; Three of Gell's captains desert; Derbyshire Royalists mustered; regiments raised and houses garrisoned

---

January 1644	—	Major Wheeler captured at Horseley; Gell isolated at Derby
5 "	—	Gell appointed governor of Derby
6 "	—	Derby horse routs Harpur at Burton
16 "	—	Newark Royalists attack Nottingham

19 "	—	Scots army invades England to assist the Parliamentarian cause
25 "	—	Battle of Nantwich; Royalist defeat
6 February	—	Derby forces storm King's Mills; Hastings's garrison surrenders
29 "	—	Second siege of Newark; Derby forces join Meldrum's besieging army
21 March "	—	Rupert relieves Newark and defeats Meldrum
29 "	—	Battle of Cheriton; Royalist defeat
31 "	—	Fight at Egginton Heath
6 May	—	Manchester's army storms Lincoln
11 June	—	Rupert takes Liverpool en route to York
2 July	—	Battle of Marston Moor; Rupert beaten
16 "	—	Surrender of York
18 "	—	Gell's forces take Wilne Ferry
28 "	—	Siege of Wingfield Manor begins; Eyre's regiment captured by Sanders at Boylestone; Bagot's men driven from Burton
2 August	—	Welbeck surrenders
12 "	—	Frescheville yields Staveley House; Bolsover surrenders to Manchester
20 "	—	Wingfield capitulates
October	—	Gell establishes a garrison at Barton to keep watch on Royalist Tutbury
20 "	—	Newcastle town falls to the Scots
27 "	—	Second Battle of Newbury; another draw
29 "	—	Newarkers defeated in cavalry fight at Denton
6 November	—	Rupert appointed overall commander of the King's remaining forces
12 "	—	Derby and Leicester Parliamentarians combine to create a garrison at Coleorton to control Ashby
19 December	—	Commons passes the Self-Denying Ordinance

January 1645	—	Sir Richard Willys governor of Newark
29 "	—	Gell arrests Major Sanders
February	—	Six troops of Derby horse serve with Brereton in the Chester leaguer and stay till April
19 February	—	Prince Maurice relieves Chester
13 March	—	Judge Advocate of the Army, Isaac Dorislaus acquits Sanders and orders his re-instatement
4 April	—	Formation of the New Model Army
7 May"	—	The King leaves Oxford with the main Royalist field army
27 "	—	The King's army encamps at Ashby
30 "	—	Royalists take Leicester by storm
14 June	—	Battle of Naseby; a Royalist disaster
16 "	—	Gell and his 2,000 horse reach Leicester
18 "	—	Lord Loughborough's garrison surrenders Leicester to Fairfax and marches to Ashby
5 July	—	Gell's horse mutinies at Sinfin Moor
10 "	—	Royalist western army defeated at Langport
16 "	—	Frescheville's men re-capture Welbeck
12 August	—	Charles arrives at Tutbury
14 "	—	Derby horse attacks Royalist rear-guard
10 September	—	Rupert surrenders Bristol to the New Model
24 "	—	Battle of Rowton Moor near Chester; King beaten
14 October	—	Storming of Basing House
15 "	—	Poyntz assembles his army at Derby to march against Newark
1 November	—	Derby horse win praise from Brereton at the Battle of Denbigh
3 "	—	Shelford House destroyed; Colonel Stanhope killed
4 "	—	John Belasyse becomes last governor of Newark
5 "	—	Wiverton taken by Parliamentarians
12 "	—	Recruiter election at Derby
13 "	—	Frescheville surrenders Welbeck to Thomas Gell
22 "	—	Derby foot storm outworks of Belvoir Castle
26 "	--	Poyntz begins third siege of Newark

---

1 January 1646	—	Derby foot attacked by Newarkers at East Stoke
14 "	--	Derby horse launch first of three attacks on Tutbury town (second on 19th, third on 26th)
3 February	—	Chester surrenders to Brereton
28 "	—	Lord Loughborough surrenders Ashby
9 March	—	Brereton begins the final siege of Lichfield Close
21 "	—	Last Royalist field army defeated at Stow on the Wold
6 April	—	Gell presents his terms to the garrison of Tutbury Castle
21 April "	—	Brereton's surrender terms accepted instead
May	—	Gell summoned to London to answer accusations

5 May	— King Charles surrenders to the Scots at Southwell
8 "	— Newark surrenders on the King's orders
24 June	— Surrender of Oxford and the end of the first Civil War
10 July	— Lichfield garrison yields to Brereton
6 September	— Gell's governorship of Derby terminated; restoration of rule by mayor and corporation
October	— Disbandment of Derby's horse and foot regiments

DERBYSHIRE ROYALISTS

Bates, Major Thomas
Bullock, Lieutenant Colonel William
Cockaine, Aston
Every, Sir Simon
Eyre, Colonel Rowland
Fitzherbert, Colonel Sir John
Frescheville, Colonel John
Harpur, Colonel Sir John
Hunloke, Lieutenant Colonel Sir Henry
Kniveton, Colonel Sir Andrew
Kniveton, Major Gilbert
Leake, Francis, Lord Deincourt
Lowe, Captain Arthur
Milward, Colonel John
Shallcross, Colonel John
Stanhope, Colonel Ferdinando
Stanhope, Colonel Philip
Stanhope, Philip, Earl of Chesterfield

ROYALISTS

Bagot, Colonel Richard, *(Staffs)*
Byron, Colonel Richard, *(Notts)*
Cavendish, William, Earl of Newcastle, *(Yorks)*
Compton, Spencer, Earl of Northampton, *(Oxford)*
Fleetwood, Sir Richard, *(Staffs)*
Goring, Major-General George, *(Yorks)*
Hastings, Henry (Lord Loughborough), *(Leics)*
Langdale, Colonel Sir Marmaduke, *(Yorks)*
Mackworth, Major-General Sir Francis, *(Yorks)*
Middleton, Captain John, *(Leics)*
Molyneux, Colonel Roger, *(Notts)*
Muschamp, Major, *(Notts)*
Prince Rupert, *(Oxford Army)*
Wheeler, Major Charles, *(Yorks)*
Whortley, Colonel Francis, *(Yorks)*
Willys, Colonel Sir Richard, *(Oxford)*

DERBYSHIRE PARLIAMENTARIANS

Ashenhurst, Captain Randle
Barton, Captain Nathaniel
Clarke, Captain Samuel
Curzon, Sir John, MP
Freland, Captain Robert
Frith, Captain William
Gell, Colonel Sir John
Gell, Lieutenant Colonel Thomas
Goring, Captain John
Greenwood, Captain Robert
Gresley, Sir George
Hadfield, Captain Thomas
Hallowes, Nathaniel, MP
Hope, Captain Robert
Mellor, Captain Robert
Molanus, Major Couradus
Mundy, Captain John
Pole, Captain German
Rhodes, Captain William
Roper, Colonel Samuel
Sanders, Major Thomas
Sleigh, Captain Samuel
Stafford, Captain Thomas
Swetnam, Captain Joseph
Taylor, Captain Samuel
Villiers, Captain
Watson, Captain Daniel

PARLIAMENTARIANS

Ballard, Major-General Thomas, *(Lincs)*
Bowyer, Colonel John, *(Staffs)*
Brereton, Sir William, *(Cheshire)*
Chadwick, Colonel James, *(Notts)*
Chadwick, Colonel Lewis, *(Staffs)*
Crawford, Major-General Lawrence, *(Eastern Association)*
Denbigh, Basil Fielding, Earl of *(Worcs)*
Essex, Robert Devereux, Earl of, *(Captain General)*
Fairfax, Sir Thomas, *(Yorks)*
Fox, Captain John, *(Warwicks)*
Greville, Robert, Lord Brooke, *(Warwicks)*
Grey, Lord Thomas, *(East Midlands Association)*
Hacker, Colonel Francis, *(Notts)*
Hartop, Sir Edward, *(Notts)*
Haughton, Colonel Robert, *(Lancs)*
Hubbard, Colonel Sir Miles, *(Lincs)*
Hutchinson, Colonel John, *(Notts)*
Hutchinson, Lucy, *(Notts)*
Ireton, Major Henry, *(Notts)*
Manchester, Earl of, *(Eastern Association)*
Meldrum, Major-General Sir John
Peyto, Lieutenant Colonel Sir Edward, *(Warwicks)*
Pierrepont, Colonel Francis, *(Notts)*
Poyntz, Colonel-General Sydenham, *(Northern Association)*
Rossiter, Colonel Sir Edward, *(Lincs)*
Shaw, Major, *(Staffs)*
Thornagh, Colonel Francis, *(Notts)*
White, Captain Charles, *(Notts)*

Battalio
Term used to describe a regiment of foot drawn up in battle order, or for formal inspection by a senior officer.

Commission of Array
An order from the King to specific notables in each county, directly summoning them to raise and recruit fighting men for the Royalist cause. Parliament contested the legality of this process and issued its Militia Ordinance to the same purpose.

Committee of Both Kingdoms
Set up by Parliament in the spring of 1644 to ensure maximum co-operation between the allied Scottish and English Parliaments in the prosecution of the war.

Compounding
An order of Parliament of April 1643 permitting local county Committees to seize or sequestrate 'delinquent' (ie Royalist) property and estates. The offending Royalist could atone for his delinquency by paying a punitive fine or composition in order to recover his property. From July 1644, this system was centralised under a special Committee sitting at Goldsmiths Hall.

Constables
Officials appointed in townships and villages to carry out the unenviable task of collecting and apportioning rates and taxes amongst the community and maintaining social order and control. During the war, they were the instruments upon whom local garrisons imposed the heavy burden of collecting contributions (q.v.).

Contributions
General term for taxes levied on localities for the upkeep of military forces.

Dragoons
Basically infantry who rode to battle and fought on foot with their muskets. They usually operated in company strength attached to the horse, and provided fire support to cavalry attacks, or in reverse, lined hedges and enclosures to beat off enemy horse.

Drake
A light field piece, smaller than a saker (q.v.) using a smaller charge of powder and having a bore that tapered at the breach end. Drakes were of two basic sizes and fired either 3lb or 6lb shot.

Foot
Name given to a body of infantry. Regiments nominally consisted of 500 to 1200 men, divided into companies, each having its own colour carried by an ensign. Soldiers were of two types — armoured pikemen with 16 foot pikes to ward off enemy horsemen, and musketeers or 'shot,' armed with cumbersome muzzle-loading matchlock muskets. These weapons could be anything up to 5 foot in length and 10lbs in weight and could fire a distance of more than 400 yards. Well drilled foot could get off perhaps two shots a minute, but the lethal range of a musket was only about 150 yards, so musketeers were trained to give volley fire as close to the enemy as possible, before wading into the foe, using the butt-ends of their muskets as clubs.

Forlorn Hope
A number of soldiers drawn out in advance of the main body, to act as a vanguard or skirmishing force, with the purpose of breaking up the cohesion of an enemy attack, or to try and sting an enemy into launching a premature advance. The term was also used to denote a storming party of picked men.

Hornworks
A military term of art for a defensive work containing artillery, jutting out from a major strongpoint.

Horse
Most Civil War horse regiments averaged some 500 troopers, organised into troops, each having their own colour carried by a cornet. Ideally, the men were equipped with back and breast-plates, worn over a buffcoat of thick leather, a helmet (usually lobster-tailed with a nose-guard) and armed with a sword and a pair of pistols. Horse were used for shock effect in combat and compared to the foot, were more expensive to raise, train, equip and supply and were mostly volunteers. Gell's muster-lists show that a horseman was entitled to an average of 15 shillings per week, whereas the humble foot soldier got 4 shillings and 8 pence. Actual receipt, of course, depended on the success or otherwise of contributions levied on surrounding communities and pay was therefore often in arrears, especially when enemy forces dominated these vital collecting-grounds.

Leaguer
Term applied to a besieging force investing the stronghold of an opponent, and usually consisting of a series of fortified camps, as at Newark and Chester.

Malignant
Disparaging term applied by Parliamentarian supporters to active Royalists, implying treachery and disloyalty to the state.

Moorlanders
Impoverished natives of the Leek area of north-east Staffordshire, who, angered by the foraging activities among them of Sir Francis Whortley's Cavalier dragoons, armed themselves with a variety of home-made weapons and marched on Royalist Stafford in February 1643. They were beaten off but joined Gell and Brereton at the battle of Hopton Heath in March. They were militarily ineffective but remained staunch supporters of the Parliament's cause.

Palisadoes
Precursors of barbed-wire entanglements, palisadoes were strong, upright, sharpened timber stakes, used in defence works to deter attackers.

Recruiter Election
Royalist term applied to Parliamentary elections held to replace Royalist MPs who had sided with the King. New MPs were 'recruited' to fill these vacancies. The election in Derby in November 1645 — to replace the Royalist William Allestrey — was a particularly acrimonious contest, between Gell's brother Thomas and Captain Robert Mellor.

Reformader/Reformadoes
Officers serving as volunteers without immediate command of troops, due to their disbandment, destruction, or having been 'reformed' into other units.

Ship Money
A pre-war device whereby Charles sought to become financially independent of Parliament. Originally a tax on coastal counties to finance naval forces in time of emergency, it was extended in 1635 to inland counties and thereby provoked a major constitutional crisis. Though abolished by the Long Parliament in July 1641, its efficient machinery of collection served as a model upon which Parliament later erected its own system of financial assessment, to pay for the war effort against the King's forces.

Trained Bands
A sort of 'Home-Guard,' comprising of part-time citizens-in-arms organised on a county basis under the Lord Lieutenant. Both sides initially tried to make use of the local trained bands as the only available reservoir of suitable manpower. However, the general reluctance of these amateur soldiers to march beyond their county boundaries, caused both Royalist and Roundhead commanders to raise regiments of volunteers instead. At Cavendish Bridge, Sawley, en route from Nottingham to Derby in September 1642, Charles inspected the Derbyshire trained bands and then promptly disarmed them in order to equip his new recruits.

Saker
Civil War artillery was far from standardised and contemporary authorities differ as to the types of ordnance they describe. Each size of gun had its own name of classification: culverin, minion, falcon, robinet etc. The saker was the most common field artillery piece, being 10½ feet in length and capable of firing a 5¼lb shot to a distance of 1,920 feet.

SOURCES

Unpublished typescript material generously supplied to the author by Dr. Brighton in 1982. Anyone with an interest in the Civil War period of Derbyshire history owes Trevor Brighton an enormous debt. His work — published and unpublished — remains unique as the only major scholarly venture into this field since the occurrence of the events themselves.

DN
Memoires of the Duke of Newcastle — Ed. C. H. Firth 1906.

DRO
Derbyshire Record Office at Matlock — contains the large Gell MSS collection (D258) in 67 boxes; the Gresley Letter Book (803M/Z9) of some 140 relevant folios and which includes the MSS 'True Account' (folios v-xvii); and the Sanders MSS collection (1232M).

Dore (1) (2)
R. N. Dore — 'The Letter Books of Sir William Brereton' Volume One, 1984 (1) and Volume Two, 1990(2).

Glover
Stephen Glover — 'The History, Gazetteer and Directory of the County of Derby' 1829. The Appendix contains the first and only publication of the Gell's 'True Relation.' Also Gresley's 'True Account' — though Gresley's original MS first appeared in Stebbing-Shaw's 'History of the Antiquities of Staffordshire' in 1798.

GLB
Gresley Letter Book — referenced by folio number (See DRO above) — maintained by Sir George Gresley whilst serving on the Derby Committee.

JBDHS
Journal of the Bakewell and District Historical Society. Co-edited by Trevor Brighton — the Journal contains almost the entirety of Brighton's output on Civil War Derbyshire:
1. The Gell family in the C16 & C17. A case of the rising gentry — January 1980 No. VII pp4-332.
2. Sir John Gell and the Civil War in Derbyshire (September 1642 to March 1643) — January 1981 No. VII pp37-63.
3. Sir John Gell Governor of Derby 1642-46 — January 1982 No. IX ppl-54.

LH
'Memoires of the Life of Colonel John Hutchinson' by Lucy Hutchinson. Edition published by OUP 1973 and edited by James Sutherland.

NCWS
Newark on Trent. The Civil War Siegeworks. HMSO 1964.

RO
'Royalist Officers in England & Wales 1642-1660' P. R. Newman. Garland 1981.

RR
'Royalists and Roundheads' by Trevor Brighton — Bakewell and District Historical Society 1981. Appendix 1 is an A to Z of Derbyshire families and their allegiances; it is essential reading for any student — in conjunction with the other 3 JBDHS volumes mentioned above.

RWE
'The Royalist War Effort in the North Midlands 1642-46.' Unpublished PhD thesis Loughborough University 1986 by Martyn Bennett, who has kindly permitted the reproduction of a number of maps and diagrams printed in RWE.

Sanders
MSS Collection of the papers of Thomas Sanders. DRO/1232M.

TA
'True Account' — 'A true account of the raising and employing of one foot regiment under Sir John Gell from the beginning of October 1642 until the middle of February 1644' by Sir George Gresley.

TR
'True Relation' — 'A True Relation on what service hath been done by Colonel Sir John Gell, bart, for the king and the parliament in defence of the town and county of Derby; and how aiding and assisting he hath been to the adjacent counties viz: Nottinghamshire, Staffordshire, Cheshire, Lancashire, Lincolnshire and Yorkshire, from October 1642 till October 1646' by Sir John Gell.

Wood
A. C. Wood "Nottinghamshire in the Civil War' Oxford 1937.

SUGGESTED FURTHER READING

P. Haythornthwaite:
  'The English Civil War 1642-1651' 1984

Keith Roberts:
  'Soldiers of the English Civil War' (1) Infantry Osprey Elite Series, 1989

John Tincey:
  'Soldiers of the English Civil War' (2) Cavalry Osprey Elite Series, 1990

P. Young & R. Holmes:
  'The English Civil Wars — A Military History' 1974

P. Young:
  'Civil War England' 1981

D. Blackmore:
  'Arms & Armour of the English Civil Wars' 1990

P. R. Newman:
  'Companion to the English Civil Wars' 1990